The Complete PupStar Guide

Sarah Bartlett KCAI CD R QIDTI

DEDICATION

For the puppies and owners who get lost, who have every best intention and get misled. To me 16 years ago, to Bella, Rosco, Ziggy, Jazz & Merlin

CONTENTS

ACKNOWLEDGMENTS

Big thanks to Lillie, Rich, Katie, Deb, Nina, Sam, Simon, Spencer & Karen for all your support and encouragement over the last few months. I wouldn't have got here without you!

1 INTRODUCTION

Firstly, thank you for not only getting your hands on this book but also for opening it! I love to share my knowledge and stories to help you. Secondly before we go any further, as a thank you gift I have lots of training videos and templates to help you and compliment what you will read, make sure you visit www.multidogmaven.co.uk/pupstarbonus to grab them, go do it now, I will be there as back up for support if needed and will know that you are on this wonderful journey with me.

This is book 2 of the Super Sidekick Series.

Book 1 is Puppy Prepared? And it gives you all you need to know about finding the right breed, breeder and puppy for you. The things you need to consider before getting a little pupster and helping you decide if it's the right call for you.

Head over to Facebook and search @SarahBartlettDogTrainer to find out more and claim your free bonuses just for purchasing this book!

What this book will/won't help you with

1st puppy, or 10th if it's a puppy in addition to existing dog or dogs you have at home currently, I strongly advise that you buy another of my books to accompany this one - 'Another Pup?' - The comprehensive guide to adding to or becoming a multi-dog household. Available direct from me or on Amazon.

Having a puppy is bloomin' hard work! And it's not all cute fluff and cuddles.

This book will give you all the knowledge, tips and tricks you need to know to mould and guide your new super sidekick, your new best friend.

It's such an exciting time when pupster comes home, a little bundle of cute. So many hopes and dreams, memories to make and adventures to have! It's also very exhausting and bloody hard work! And even with lots of effort and all the best intentions there will be times where you question yourself. Moments of 'did I do the right thing?' moments of 'I really love them, but god life was so much easier without them'.

This is normal!

Even I go through this with every pup I have had, and I have had 8 puppies of my own over the last 16 years.

You may have friends with dogs or even with puppies and you look at them and think they are so good and you feel deflated at your pup's antics. You start to wonder what you have done wrong, that you must be a really bad pet parent!

Stop right there!

Struggles, sleepless nights, worry, anxiety and panic are all normal - within reason of course.

You are an amazing pet parent who wants to get it right! After all you wouldn't be here reading my words if you weren't, and I promise you I will guide you to getting the dog of your dreams no matter how it may feel right now.

I can waffle on at times but that's only to help you understand the what's and whys of things and to ensure you are on the right path, the path to success with your new best friend.

How to use this book

If you have just brought pup home or about to then start reading through from the beginning.

If you are struggling and pup has been home for a few weeks then refer to the index for the key words of what you are struggling with and go from there, also look at the chapter for the life stage/age they are at.

Don't forget to visit the exercise (Page 85) and socialisation (Page 9) sections, getting these two key factors right will make all the difference I promise!

What this book won't help with

If you have bought a breed that is totally unsuitable for your lifestyle or personality/routine or you don't have the time to invest into ensuring an easier life for both of you.

Yes, you will find lots of tips and tricks in here that will help in these situations, but sometimes we can all get it wrong. I have got it wrong many times and it's shaped me to be the dog trainer and owner I am today. I have adjusted my work and life to adapt along the way but I also recognise that not everyone can do that. I accept there are types and breeds of dogs that would never be suitable for me and my lifestyle. Even with my knowledge and experience I accept that no matter how I may admire that breed or type of dog I know they would not be a good fit.

Beware of Numpty Advice

The dangers of Dr Google, YouTube, Facebook keyboard warriors and

'Uncle Fred' who has always had dogs

With all the advice out there nowadays around dog training, puppy raising and ownership it's hard to know what to believe, who to follow and know what is best for you and your pupster.

YouTube, TV programs, friends and family all have their own two penneth to put in and it becomes a minefield of confusion!

Confusion not just for you but for puppy as you try one thing and then try another and another and nothing really gives the results you want; you wonder why and who to ask next or give up entirely.

The dangers of each type of possible numpty advice

Uncle Fred (the dog man who has always had dogs and knows best).
It may not be an uncle, it may be a neighbour or friend, but we all know that one person who appears to know dogs and have well trained pooches so of course you will listen to them, why wouldn't you? You trust them and you can see the results.

There are a couple of things to consider here - they have likely had a few of the same breed of dog over the years and know that breed, a breed that is unlikely to be the same as what you have got, and they are different no matter how much Uncle Fred tells you dogs are dogs, believe me they are not. Breed and breed type matters and makes a big difference.

Times have moved on a lot since they got their first dog, and while they might make it work for their dog science and training is a world away from what it was 15 years ago, which could be just since they got their last puppy.

Not meaning to be crude here but I will always be straight with you - if you have had female genitalia all of your life it doesn't make you a gynaecologist! Read that again, and let it sink in.

That's not to say you need to be rude when advice is offered from

Uncle Fred, be polite and thank them for their input, then forget what they say!

YouTube

While yes there are good, modern, reward-based trainers on YouTube there are also many cowboys who claim to be one thing and give dangerous advice that could ruin your bond with your dog. The problem being you won't know what's good and bad and that's how they get under your skin. Many of these cowboys are very good at marketing but lack the depth of knowledge needed for true modern dog training to give you and pup the best foundation.

Facebook / social media groups and so-called experts

You find everyone is an expert when they hide behind a keyboard and how do you know if they are who they say they are on social media, you can claim to be the world's best dog trainer, breeder, vet etc. and the oracle on all things dog and no one will question it, if they have the time to be answering everyone's questions on social media about dogs, what do they do in their normal life? Unless the group is run by a pro trainer that you know and trust and it's the trainer replying then how do you know that the advice being given is correct?

There are many ways to skin a cat, and there are many methods of dog training out there. That's not to say that another trainer who does things differently is wrong or isn't knowledgeable it's just we all have our own way of learning and teaching things. Dogs have different learning styles just as humans do.

The key thing to remember is that the most modern and up to date training is science based and positive and builds resilience and confidence in a dog. Anything that's punishment-based, shouting at, forcing, hitting or breaking the spirit of the dog is very outdated and not needed. I get that it maybe how you have grown up with the family dog's training, but times move on, just like we don't have the cane or corporal punishment in schools anymore.

We certainly do not need to show puppy who is boss! We don't need to ensure we eat before them or pin them down or not allow them on the bed because they may become aggressive.

There has been a train of thought in dog training for a number of years now that we need to be dominant over our dogs, this is just not true. One way to make any trainer worth their salt to see red is to mention 'dominance' or 'show them who's boss'.

The oxford dictionary definition of dominance – to have control or influence over others.

We decide when our dog's toilet, eat, sleep, play and exercise - if that isn't control and influence over them, I don't know what is. We don't need to make a point of being dominant over our dogs because we are naturally; they live with us and have to work around our lifestyles, routines and habits. As I type now, I'm in bed and Ripple and Moss (two of my Dachshunds) are on the bed sleeping, happy and content. They don't sit there like Pinky and the Brain and plot to take over the world because I let them come on the bed from time to time or if I happen to feed them before me.

My personal view on the partnership with our dogs is exactly that, a partnership. It's mutual respect, understanding and us calmly guiding them to make the right choices, setting them up for success in training and life. We are our dog's advocate; we protect them when needed and they keep up their end of the deal by being our companions and family members. By being the constant companion. The best friend we need when we are low and who to go on walks with and make memories and grow with. I know I am a different person to the 18 year old that collected my little Ziggy at 8 weeks, 15 years on a lot has changed in my life, highs, lows, trauma and achievements. That little lad has been with me at every step and we are life partners.

You have invested time and money into this book so you can get it right - massive pat on the back to you! Seriously, I'm not being condescending here. That's a massive step to ensure you get it right - more happy dogs and happy owners can only be a good thing.

There will be times that you start to wonder why you got a puppy... Yes really! This is going to happen and when it does you should know this is normal and natural and even I go through it with each new puppy I add to my family. Their hormones kick in after those initial sleepy, totally cute first few weeks, we become tired of their abundant energy and our patience wains. We start to think we have got it wrong and wonder if we did the right thing.

I promise you; you will have these moments!

What we want to avoid, is this becoming more than just fleeting moments and becoming recurring thoughts over months and then you having to make the hard decision to give the dog up or live the next ten to fifteen years in misery with the wrong dog for you.

The sad truth is this happens all the time. We all have the best intentions but often our initial excitement of getting a puppy and our lack of thought and research leads to misery.

Why should you listen to me?

I have done it all wrong. I have paid the price, and unfortunately so have some of my dogs as I went along. I speak from experience, heart-breaking experience at times and I want to help you avoid all the things I had to go through so you can get it right first time.

Who the hell am I to tell you what you should and shouldn't do?

I have had 8 puppies of my own (not including ones I have bred) over the last 16 years, plus an additional 6 adult dogs not from pups. I am currently owned by 3 dogs and a pony; I was at 6 dogs, a pony and a cat until recently. We sadly lost our goon, the Flatcoat Retriever that was Merlin and our old cat Dobi in 2019, I left my marriage in October of 2020 leaving two dogs behind and keeping three with me - Ziggy now 15 years old, Moss 9 and Ripple is 3. They are all miniature longhaired Dachshunds though I have to say while yes, I absolutely adore my Dachs and miss the other two (another Dach and a Springer), I am very much a big dog person! I had waited 18 months for a Flatcoat Retriever puppy and managed to be there for part of the litter being born but it isn't the right time for me to raise a flatty, the more you progress through this book the more you will understand. I am gutted that I have missed out this time and while yes, I know I would make do and somehow manage to raise a flatty while trying to get my life back on track it's not ideal and it would put a lot of pressure on me. I wouldn't be able to finish this book right now if I had a little baby goon at my feet! So, I am waiting another 18 months for my dufus.

I spend my days training dogs and their owners, most of these are puppies which is what has led me to write this book and the rest of the series.

I won't bore you with the long list of courses, workshops and seminars I have attended over the years, nor go through the thousands of dogs and owners I have helped over the last 14 years of running my business but those things along with my own experiences and failures have given me the know how to show and guide you through that first year with your little land shark and help you mould them into a PupStar.

2 CORRECT SOCIALISATION

In my view and experience there are many more dogs dying (being euthanised) due to not being socialised at a young enough age which in turn causes behaviour issues than there are being put to sleep due to not being vaccinated and have contracted a core disease.

This is your choice, I am not advising either way on this matter. Only asking for you to consider further and I will share my own experiences on it.

Professionally I see far too many puppies that have only come home from the breeders and been to the vets and back a couple of times before 12 weeks of age.

These puppies turn out to have fears and phobias of many things outside of the house because they were not exposed to them often and in a in a positive way under 12 weeks of age. This often causes serious behaviour issues that last a lifetime.

I do recognize that people with the perfect puppy are less likely to call me; most people who ask for help from a professional are experiencing issues with their puppy or dog. I will always see the negative side more than the positive.

This really saddens me when it could so easily be avoided. Owners will follow the advice of 'not allowing them out till a week after the puppy course of vaccinations are complete' at best this means puppy is allowed out at 11 weeks and at worst with one course of vaccinations this can be as late as 15 weeks.

No vet should administer a vaccination to an unhealthy dog. What if your pup contracts a tummy bug and this postpones vaccinations by a week? A week may not seem like a lot, but it truly is when at such an impressionable age.

The optimum socialisation period is from 3-12 weeks. For some breeds such as Labradors this can go on until 16 weeks. During this time the more short positive experiences they can have with the big wide world the better. Different types of people, traffic, pushchairs, wheelchairs, horses, other species, weather, sounds, smells the better. The key thing to remember is short periods of exposure, positive (if they are not scared) and with plenty of opportunity to sleep/rest between new experiences. Socialisation to the world is the most important thing and should be prioritised above all else while in this age bracket, they can learn to sit and wait, etc. later. Correct socialisation can be the difference between a lifelong happy, well-rounded companion or an insecure or aggressive shaking wreck. After 12 weeks, socialisation should continue for months if not years but what pup learns in the initial window is the basis for everything else.

If you are bringing puppy home at 8 weeks it's worth keeping in mind that you can take them to friends' houses... after all the puppy could have gone to its new home in any of those houses, how is it any different?

Carrying your puppy out and about letting it see traffic, people, wheelie bins etc. is not putting it at risk of infection, it is in your arms, not on the floor. Taking it for regular short trips in the car is very beneficial also.

Short positive experiences with new things while still under 12 weeks will really help you bond and have a confident happy dog for years to come. Buy a carrier or pouch if needed. This is harder with larger breeds so a stroller maybe a better option.

Short and Positive being the key words here. Just 15 minutes going somewhere new each day will make a big difference.

Initial fear period - worth noting!

Puppies will go through a natural stage in their development at around 8 weeks of age.

It's a stage in which they become spooked by things they were previously ok with; this can last for a day or up to a week. Some pups will go through this stage before 8 weeks some after, but the average is 8 weeks. Keep this in mind when they are experiencing what are essentially some very drastic changes, being taken from mother, littermates and its familiar environment. Have patience with them when they settle in at home with you. If you notice them becoming scared maybe just spend a couple of days at home with them before then taking them out to meet the world again, so they don't get more fearful of things. This phase passes very quickly.

The big misunderstanding when it comes to socialisation

Socialising a puppy the right way means putting more importance on the environment, the weather, traffic, different types of people, pushchairs, trolleys, noises, smells, sights, different surfaces – the human world and all it entails.

There is a big misconception that puppy must meet every dog it comes across – this isn't the case and will not help you in future as puppy grows.

It's crucial that your pup learns to walk past other dogs calmly, to not be worried about other dogs of all breeds but playing lots with other dogs is not the way to do this.

Ideally, we want your puppy to meet 'boring' older role model dogs. And a range of breeds including short muzzled breeds, breeds with upright and droopy ears, small and large, fluffy and short coat, short or no tail as well as curly tail dogs and straight tail dogs. Also, black dogs. The range of what a dog is and looks like and behaves is vast, so ensuring your pup can read all of these types and not be worried by them is important – but not learning they are more fun than you!

Most importantly socialisation is about getting them used to and confident around everything they will be expected to cope with throughout their life.

To play or not to play that is the question

Humans playing with dogs with toys and food? Yes, yes, yes!!

Don't forget it's so important that we bond with our dogs more than they bond with each other.

Letting them play with each other? Hmm, not a great idea on the whole.

Do my dogs play with each other? Yes
Do they play all the time? No
Do they play every day? No
Do they play with other dogs outside of the household? Very rarely and only with dogs I and they know well.

If you let your pup play with dogs continually it can and in most cases will cause an issue. You will end up with a dog who runs off to see other dogs all the time on walks, who prefers another dog's company to you and who will likely get bitten at some point by a dog who does not appreciate it and your dog may end up being fearful or aggressive towards other dogs as a result.

From a health and development perspective play can cause real damage to your puppy's growing form. An injury is so easy at a young age as their skeleton is so soft, almost like jelly. Differences in size and weight between puppy and adult dog needs to be a real factor for consideration here.

One of the biggest problems I see is a puppy who has played lots with dogs when younger or has played lots with the other dog or dogs in the household then as it grows starts to get frustrated and wants to get to other dogs all the time. Often pulling and lunging on the lead. They don't understand why they can't 'go and say hi' to every dog it sees now it's bigger when it was allowed to before.

Young pups going to day care establishments or being on group walks with the dog walker can cause issues for you too if they are not managed correctly.

See chapter 9 page 65 for more on socialisation with other dogs.

3 PET PROFESSIONALS & HOLIDAY CARE

Holiday care for pup?

An expensive do normally, but our furry family members are worth every penny to ensure they are safe when we cannot be there. While many people rely on family and friends to care for their dog while they are away, what if they are also away or their circumstances change over your dog's lifetime? It is likely they will. We are talking around 15 years - lots can change. You can never take a break away with these friends or family members without the dog if they are usually the ones to care for your dog.

Home boarders and kennels

Home boarders and kennels in England must be licensed which also helps to ensure the safety of your beloved pet so please check with your local authority who is and isn't licensed.

Most local authorities will stipulate as part of the licensing that your dog must be up to date with their core vaccinations plus the kennel cough vaccine. For both of these options always check how long your dog will have human companionship each day, how long they will be exercised for, how they will be exercised and if they will need to be in the company of other dogs.

Home boarding is where your dog goes to stay in a dog professionals' home and cared for as part of their family.

Sometimes home boarders may have their own dogs too, or other dogs staying so most home boarding agreements will require your dog to be sociable with other dogs.

Pet sitters

This consists of a pet carer living in your house while you are away. It's often the most expensive option for one dog but normally cheaper than kennelling when you have multiple animals. This option ensures additional security for the home and also means the animals are kept in their normal environment. Check how long they will be left alone for as often pet sitters will go to walk other dogs etc. in the day.

Pet care professionals & Services – A word of warning

Dog walkers, trainers, pet sitters, kennels, day care establishments, home boarders and groomers - none of these industries are regulated.

Seriously! There is no governing body to ensure that they adhere to a minimum standard of care, knowledge or experience.

There are slightly more rules for home boarders, day care establishments and kennels to adhere to with the recent addition to the licensing laws for these professional services. Firstly - check if they are licensed and to what level, you will be able to find this information on their local council website.

In 14 years of business this is one thing that still saddens me and has done from the start.

Yes, I provide many of the services listed above or have done in the past if not now.

What saddens me about this industry is that it remains to this day, unregulated. This is not just dog walkers; it applies to trainers, groomers, day care establishments and much more. There has been talk of regulating it for years, but it is just that - talk. We are caring for your precious family members and in the wrong hands it can, and often does end in disaster. This then paints the rest of us with the same brush. Over the past five years I have noticed many, many people start up as a dog walking enterprise and while some will stick at it and do good things, the majority either give up or worse they do not educate themselves in dog language, the law and dog management and make mistakes. We are all human and we all make mistakes but not ensuring you are knowledgeable in your field is ignorance, and in some cases, arrogant.

'Just because someone is insured and CRB checked it does not mean they are 'qualified' to care for your dog in any capacity'.

Dogs die in the care of so-called professionals every day. They are beaten, hit and kicked behind closed doors. And their behaviour can deteriorate from a simple lack of skills and knowledge on the pet care provider's part. I don't mean to scare you with this, but it is worth being very aware of this. After-all, you have spent the time and money in investing in your puppy; you wanted to get it right from the start. Substandard care can quickly undo all of your hard work.

Most pet owners will need to use a pet care provider at some point over their pet's lifetime, please do your research, and get to know them before handing over your precious family member.

You can Google Professional dog walker guidelines UK.

There are no hard fast rules. As I said before this is not regulated but it is something you should be looking at when employing a pet carer and questioning if they adhere to these guidelines. They may not be aware of them, but you can ask how they do or don't do certain things using the guide as an outline.

Dog trainers and behaviourists

Again, sadly no regulation. There are hundreds if not thousands of membership schemes and organisations that portray themselves to be governing bodies that professionals can join. If you see that the trainer you are looking at is affiliated with an organisation, usually this is by letters, an acronym either after their name or stated on their website. Then check out the organisation and their own website. Look at their code of practice that your trainer has signed up to and what the process is to become accredited with them, if they are in fact accredited and not just a student member and if their beliefs in training are aligned with your own. For practice check out who I am with - the KCAI (kennel club accredited instructor) and QIDTI (qualified international dog training instructor).

If nothing else do your research, ask for recommendations, look for reviews online etc.

Dog training classes

It has now been proven that taking your puppy to puppy training classes are beneficial to your dog's overall behaviour throughout its lifetime (I have to add, that the right class is key here).

Taking your puppy along to classes may cost more than a walk in the park or a run along the beach, but researchers have revealed that it helps to make them more confident animals in their adult life.

The study found that those pups who were taken to six weekly classes were able to cope better with strangers, grew up better behaved and were less stressed.

Picking the right classes for you and your puppy is important. Go and watch a class first without your puppy. Watch who the trainers help, is it the best dogs that they spend more time with or the ones who need the help the most? How many dogs are in the class and how many trainers are there, what's the ratio? A small numbered class with more than one trainer is ideal.

Are the trainers offering/teaching more than one way to do things? If they only know one way to teach something this isn't a sign of a knowledgeable trainer.

Do you like the trainer? If you don't like them then you are not likely to pay attention and learn much from them. A little like, we always do better at school in the classes and subjects where we like the teacher.

If a class or training club does not want you to come and watch first then they are not worth wasting your time and money on.

Often the best classes are fully booked in advance so you may need to do this research before puppy comes home to ensure you can get on the list and get to classes at the right time.

4 COLLECTING PUPPY – THE BIG DAY

Do a safety check before you leave home

Areas of the house / safety

Consider where you will want your dog to go and not go. No, your dog does not need to be able to go in every single room in the house. If you want that, that's fine but I would suggest you consider puppy housetraining, fouling on expensive rugs, carpets and the possibility of them chewing your beloved furniture. Even if you wish for your dog to have free roam when they are an adult, they do not need to have free roam when they are a puppy and in fact restricting access to certain areas will make your life a lot easier and in turn make it easier to train your puppy. I will speed up the house/toilet training process too. My own dogs are not allowed free roam of the house, in fact 90% of the time they are restricted to our open plan kitchen, living room, diner and conservatory. These are the areas we spend the most time too so it's not as if they are shut out away from us all of the time. Carpets are upstairs, with hard flooring downstairs (handy for tiny bladders in case of any accidents), electric cables are either hidden or behind furniture without such a gap that a puppy could get behind them. You are not being mean by restricting your puppy to the kitchen or utility area, particularly if you are not around – this is damage limitation and setting you both up for success.

Things puppies love but we don't like them to love

Electric cables
Wood – chair legs etc.
Skirting board corners
TV remotes
Rugs
Slippers/shoes
Our hands
Our feet
Fluffy dressing gowns and any item of clothing that flaps around
Sofa corners
Wicker baskets, chairs etc.
Cushions
Paper/books/DVD cases
Anything that is left on the floor or within reach!!

In your puppy's eyes, everything is there to investigate and chew!
EVERYTHING!

So, no matter how many toys and chews you buy for your pup they will still find something else to grab, chew, bite or wee on that you don't want them to. The more we restrict what they can get to that they shouldn't the better!

Short term, the tidier you can be with putting things away etc. the better! You may need to think about temporarily boarding/blocking off little holes or gaps behind the TV if you have one on a TV stand, pushing sofas back to walls if you have plugs behind, taking up rugs etc.

You can get 'anti-chew' sprays to spray on things like soft furnishings and chair and table legs etc. to discourage chewing. I have only found one such product that has the desired results for most if not all dogs. In 14 years of working with hundreds if not thousands of puppies and having my own for 16 years I have found that 'Grannicks bitter apple spray' is the most reliable but two puppies I have worked with have not been put off by it. Most if not all brands from mainstream pet shops I have found a less that 50% success rate so always recommend Grannicks. It's available on

Amazon. Google will suggest various home remedies such as lemon juice, curry powder etc. - again mixed results.

I would not simply rely on a spray to avoid damage. Sprays are more of an added extra with management being the number one thing. I didn't need to use Grannicks at all when raising Ripple as we had cracked the management and provided plenty of mental stimulation, chews, toys and training to keep her occupied and tired.

Using management/prevention is great and very important but we also need to provide puppy with things they are allowed to chew, I'm not just talking about toys either. Puppies NEED to chew, as do adult dogs, but puppies in particular. It's not just a want for them it's a need, and more so when they are teething which starts from 12 weeks and finishes at around 6 months. Chewing is a stress reliever and a pain reliever; it helps to tire them out mentally and provides great enrichment. The more we can provide tasty things for them to chew the less likely they are to apply their chewing instinct to things we would rather they didn't. Having a good supply of chews, stuffed Kongs and even home-made items for them to chew on is vital in this. Yes, they can chew on their toys also but providing something tasty makes them both less likely to want to chew items they shouldn't and helps to prevent the toy destruction too.

Safety check complete? Time to go and collect your new bestie!

Try and arrive at the breeder's house as early in the day as possible to collect puppy so they have a full day to settle in their new home with you.

When you go to collect puppy

A reminder that you should collect, and if the breeder is offering to deliver puppy or meet you somewhere this is not a good breeder and to avoid!

The breeder should give you the following:

- Their vaccination card as they should have had their first vaccination of the initial course
- Feeding instructions
- Worming details
- Registration certificates if applicable
- Most breeders will give you four weeks free insurance
- Their microchip details
- Puppy sales contract that you and the breeder sign
- Receipt for the money to purchase puppy
- A week's supply of food
- Your puppy of course!

The journey home

You should pack cleaning supplies in case of any accidents on route, a blanket, hot water bottle/heat source and ideally someone else to drive you. Take a collar and lead to fit puppy for emergencies (and their tag so you are abiding by the law). If the breeder can give you a blanket or towel smelling of the litter that would be perfect, if not take a towel or similar to rub all over mum and pups, so the scent of the blanket or towel you will have on your lap in transport will be familiar and comforting to puppy.

If you are travelling a long way to and from the breeders then you may need to stop somewhere to let puppy toilet on the way home. Try and find somewhere where it's unlikely to have had lots of dogs there and try not to put pressure on the collar and lead when doing this. Let them explore safely and you will find that they will do their business fairly quickly if you have been travelling for more than an hour. This should be a brief stop to get them home asap.

If they are upset with travelling, provided you have another person driving, have them on your lap in their blanket and comfort them.

Just because their first journey with you is on your lap does not mean they will expect this to be forever. This is about making this part as easy as possible for them to ensure you are bonding from the start.

If you have to go alone then ensure you have a crate or similar that is dark (maybe a blanket over) and fixed ideally on the passenger seat so you can talk to them to reassure them on route.

5 WELCOMING THEM HOME & SURVIVING THE FIRST NIGHT

Arrival home

Puppy will need to toilet so take straight into the garden and praise verbally when they perform (try and wait to speak until they have finished going to the toilet, not during the act so as to not interrupt or distract them).

*If you have other animals, pets etc. please keep them out of the way for a while, maybe a couple of hours while puppy gets used to its new environment.

*If it is a cold day, or you have a cold house you may need to be brief outside or put the heating up for a few days. Young puppies often struggle to regulate their temperature and if they are cold, they will be more unsettled, mouthing and less likely to sleep well.

Once toileting has been complete, bring them into the house, offer them a drink. The stress of travelling will have made them thirsty. They may not drink straight away, but at least they know where to find water for later. Let them explore in their own time – the prime opportunity for you to make yourself a drink and sit down while watching them from a distance. Once they have explored depending on the time of day, they may need feeding, feed them in their pen or area they will be expected to sleep in, etc. Toilet trip outside again.

Pups need to sleep a lot so you may find they collapse in a heap before too long, let them.

Place them in their pen to sleep ideally with something warm such as a microwavable pet safe heat pad or a hot water bottle wrapped in a towel; they should rest for a while.

*If you have young children its best that they are either out with family for a couple of hours or that you have given them something to do and they are not trying to interact with puppy just yet.

It's a very stressful time for puppy to leave all it has ever known, its mother, its brothers and sisters, the breeder, the smells, noises that were all so familiar to come to a very new and somewhat alien place with new people, sight, sounds and smells.

Once they are asleep you can not only take pictures of your new cute little family member but also start to sort the paperwork that the breeder gave you.

You should have their crate/pen set up already.

When it comes to feeding time follow the instructions as given by the breeder and feed them in their pen or crate with the door shut. Open the door just before they have finished eating.

Trips out to the garden should be every 20/30 minutes while they are awake and after each event they wake up, they have eaten, had a play session with you, met someone new etc. Always go with them into the garden. There will be accidents, and this is ok! You are still getting used to each other and learning how to read each other and communicate.

Over the course of the first day, there should be lots of sleeping, small doses of playing, short sessions in their crate/pen, exploring and eating.

The first night

I get more emails, calls and messages about this than anything else from new puppy owners.

It really is like having a new-born baby and you should be getting up in the night. But not for months!

Firstly, we need to ensure puppy's needs are met before we expect them to settle. They should have been to the toilet, they should not be hungry, they should have played and be tired and they should have a warm comfy place to sleep.

Unless you have found the best breeder in the world who had started to ensure pups were sleeping apart from each other before you collected them then we need to remember that puppies in the litterbox will pile on top of each other to sleep. They will keep each other warm and they will be feeling/hearing each other's heartbeats. They are not going to have that now and their sleep will not be as deep for the first few nights as they adjust. We can help them though! We can mimic the heat and the heartbeats. And we can make what is a traumatic transition, easier for them and for our sanity!

How can we help them adjust to not having a heap of puppies to curl up with and to learn to sleep away from you?

The main things we need to help them are to cover three areas - smell, heat and sound/feel.

There is a product on the market that provides all of these in one and something that I love. It's called a snuggle puppy. It's a small soft toy shaped like a dog, it has a fake heartbeat mechanism inside, and you can place heat packs in there too. A brilliant invention, I have two!

Don't worry there are alternatives to this –

- A ticking clock or watch – wrapped in a blanket or towel.

- A pet safe microwaveable heat pad or hot water bottle (wrap in a blanket so it's not too hot).
- A soft toy for them to curl up with – not a child's soft toy as the stuffing is often toxic to dogs, this should be a dog toy.
- Ideally the blanket you brought home with you that smells of the litter/mum.

Ensure puppy has eaten, has been to the toilet and is tired before placing in their sleep area with items as above that will help them settle.

I would expect some mild whining and whinging at this point, for a few minutes. Stick around, make yourself the last drink, read a chapter of a book etc. so you are nearby.

Ignoring a little whining isn't going to harm puppy, as hard as it may be. Please try your hardest not to look at them when they do this or talk to them (looking, talking and touching are all forms of reward and this will encourage them to carry on). If all goes well, they will soon settle and go to sleep, this is your cue to leave them and go to bed.

If you find that they are panicking, screaming and distressed (this is very different to whining, a bit of yapping and whinging) then simply, calmly and quietly take them out into the garden and see if they need to toilet, this is often due to them needing something when they panic, try and address their needs and then start again with trying to get them to settle.

You may want to use ear plugs for this stage but ensure that you can still hear them if they panic as **they should not be left to panic**, you should **go and help** them if they are distressed to this extent.

Take note of the time that they go to sleep and set an alarm for in around 3-4 hours You are aiming to wake them up to take them to toilet in the middle of the night rather than them learning to wake you or managing to toilet in their sleep area.

Wake them take them into the garden and praise them for doing their business, ensure they have some heat still in their sleep area and place them back to sleep again. Repeating the settle routine as before.

Set your alarm for either your time to get up or for 3 hours' time, whichever is sooner.

You will not be getting up in the middle of the night for very long, a couple of weeks maybe.

As long as you are successful in waking them up before they wake you up. As the nights progress put your alarm on for 10 to 15 minutes later each night and before you know it (and before you become too much of a zombie), your pup will not only be sleeping through the night, but they will also be holding their tiny bladders overnight too.

If they do manage to wake you before you them then again as long as it's not the all-out panic and it's just a little cry, try to leave them until they are quiet for two whole minutes before going down to them and taking them out. The 2 minute rule is important, and you will learn more about this in the frustrations and tantrums section on page 56.

If they do manage to have an accident in this time, don't worry too much. You should have spare bedding if it's in their bedding or if you have the pen and crate set up, they should have puppy pads or newspaper or similar to toilet on in the pen area if they are caught short.

Patience, time and practice

You will be tired, there will be times you wondered why you did this, but this is all normal and it will pass quickly as long as you are setting them up for success.

Puppy just wants to play and gets very distracted in the garden?

At least until we are 90% housetrained, I do not tend to play with puppy in the garden much if at all. This is so they don't think it's a big playground. I do not let them stay outside alone/unsupervised so they can't go find things to do that they shouldn't (picking up stones, digging etc.), supervision until they are older and can be trusted more.

If puppy has not performed after 10-15 minutes in the garden, then I will bring them back in and confine them in their pen for a short period before trying again. If your puppy is getting very distracted and excited and showing no signs of wanting to toilet when in the garden, then it's worth introducing the lead and taking them out on the lead and slowly walking them around the garden till they go.

See page127 for further house and crate training tips.

Puppy plan and paperwork?

You will need to set aside an hour or two in the first 48 hours to sort paperwork and a plan.

Contract and receipt – file these away safe. You may need to refer to them in future and you may need the receipt for the insurance in future.

KC Registration documents or Mix Breed Club registration documents (common for poodle hybrids that have been responsibly bred) – You will need to read through these documents and apply to have the pup be registered in your name now rather than the breeders. With the Kennel Club there is a fee of around £15 for the 'transfer of ownership' which you can either do online or by post. You will be given options to purchase five generation certificates as an additional cost, this is your choice but isn't essential.

Microchip – You will need to register your details with the

microchip company rather than the breeders. There may be a small charge for this.

Insurance – The breeder should have activated a free 4 week policy for you before you leave their property if they have offered insurance. In such cases you don't need to do anything with this straight away. You will often receive correspondence in the first week from them, confirming cover and offering a lowered rate for you to take out a policy with them before the free cover ends. It's worth doing your research and shopping around for ongoing cover. Also, it's worth speaking to the vets to ask if they have had insurance companies refuse to pay out for claims. I recommend a pet insurance broker called VIP who can advise and help you without any additional charges.

Vets

You should always get your puppy checked out at the vets once they are settled and ideally in the first 5 days of bringing them home, this is to check their health and wellbeing as much as start to get them used to the environment.

A note if your breeder has already ensured first vaccines have been administered before your pup comes home

This is common practice amongst most responsible breeders. However, many new pup owners experience problems with this.

The breeder has been responsible by starting vaccinations and passed the vaccination certificate to the new owners when they take puppy home with them. Puppy owners then take puppy to the vet for their second set of jabs only to be met with resistance from the vet. Many vets will use different brands and vaccine protocols, some only advising two vaccinations for a puppy course some up to four according to the manufacturer's instructions. If your vet does not use the same brand as the brand used already on your puppy then often a new course is the advice from the vet to be started from scratch. This presents a double risk to your puppy. The first risk being over vaccination (increased likelihood of side effects which can sometimes be behaviour issues not just physical health). The second risk, postponing the time from which your vet deems it safe for your puppy to meet the world and are classed as fully vaccinated. If you come across this situation, I would advise you to call around your local vets to see if they use the same brand as what your puppy has already had. This does not mean you need to use the same vet for the dog's lifetime if you do not want, merely just use them for their puppy vaccinations. Finding a vet that uses the same brand and protocols as what you have already used is the simplest solution to a very common problem.

Spending some time ensuring puppy can continue the course that the breeder started can mean you can enjoy taking pup out and socialising them in their optimum window up to four weeks earlier than if you start a different course from scratch. The importance of this is far reaching and can be the difference between a happy confident adult dog and a dog who is scared of the world.

Next item on the agenda

Enrolling in a puppy class or private training help - worth its weight in gold for the right one!

Dog training classes

Often the best classes are fully booked in advance so you may need to research before puppy comes home to ensure you can get on the list and get to classes at the right time.

Private training help

Classes may not be convenient for you, and that is ok. It's worth considering asking for private help from a trainer, they can come out to you a few days after pup comes home to ensure you are both forming the right habits and preventing possible future issues. Even at 8 weeks they are not too young to learn what to do and not to do.

In fact, the earlier you start the easier they are to train. Young puppies are little learning sponges, constantly learning whether we want them to or not they are learning about you, their surroundings, what works and what doesn't. Look for a trainer who is qualified, has a good reputation, has had more than one puppy of their own over the years and who you can get on with. A trainer who uses positive motivational methods is a must and certainly a question to ask when you speak to them initially.

Puppy Parties

Vets will often offer puppy parties; these are rarely a good thing for your puppy. My best advice is to say thanks but no thanks!

The premise of these events is that you can take your puppy to socialise with other puppies while they wait to be allowed out after vaccinations are complete and get a good experience at the vets. On face value this must be a positive thing and while some are run correctly unfortunately it is the minority. In reality most cases the puppies learn only to be bullied or how to be a bully to others and this is a pattern that is then set for life. Vets and veterinary nurses are very well educated in animal illnesses, symptoms, treatments and medications they are often not well educated in training and behaviour. A well run one does not allow free play between puppies and instead encourages confidence building around objects and toys etc. with some basic training, while being in the same room as other puppies.

Final item to sort is your plan

Where are you going or not going for the next few days? What positive situations will you be exposing your puppy to and how many visitors will you have? You can grab your socialisation plan template for free here - www.multidogmaven.co.uk/pupstarbonus

6 THE FIRST WEEK – HARD WORK!

Remember that puppy will want and need to sleep a lot if not most of the time in the first week that you bring them home. Make the most of it. This phase is gone before you know it!

The most important things to concentrate on in the first week are:

- Housetraining
- Teaching them their name
- Bonding
- Ensuring they get enough rest
- Mouthing
- Introduce the collar
- Forming good habits

Let them settle for the first 2-3 days and then start their socialisation program at their pace and considering their confidence. Also after the first 3 days start getting them used to being left alone (safely) for very short periods.

Keep a housetraining/activity diary!

This will really help you to make progress.

For example:

Day 1 – wee and poo 7am in garden.
7.30, accidents by back door etc.

Make a note of what times you have fed them, if you had a visitor or a delivery, if the kids came home from school or from grans etc. This will help you see a pattern and help you shape a great routine that is specific to you and your puppy.

Ripple's diary for our first 48 hours:

Day 1

After walking our adult dogs, we arrived at the breeder's house (20 minutes away) late morning and left an hour later. Ripple travelled on my lap with a blanket smelling of littermates and a snuggle pup (fake heartbeat). No whining or crying while travelling, relaxed, happy to be held.

Arrive home, take her straight into the garden and she had a wee. After letting the adult dogs out to toilet (separate to Ripple) they were shut away with frozen Kongs to let Ripple acclimatise.

Feed in pen, shut in pen and ignored for a short period.
Two wees in the garden.
Two periods of sleep.
3:00 pm adult dog's toilet/garden access for a short period without coming into contact with Ripple.
Exposure to the cat and household noises (hoover, dishwasher, coffee machine, etc.)
Two more wees in the garden
One more sleep
Introductions to the dogs, individually 4:30 – 5:00 pm
Chew bones all around 5:05 pm
Sleep at 5:20 pm
6:00 pm awake and wee
10 minute play
6:30 pm sleep in my arms

8:00 pm feed and wee
Adult dogs are milling around while Ripple is in pen and they are in the same room.
Sleep
10:30 pm awake, quick play session
Outside but no toilet 10:45 pm
Tried to play, too tired put in pen 11:10 pm with a few treats in a Kong
Settled/asleep 11:40 pm
3:30 am wee

Notes: Shivering when outside, and not getting warm very quickly when returned indoors. Using microwaveable heat pad in the pen and plan to use in a soft crate when traveling. No poo, slightly worried but bright in herself, not dehydrated, hope she will do one in the night or the morning, if not - call the breeder and visit vet.

Day 2

7:00 am wee and feed
7:15 am first poo (never been so happy to see a puppy poo!)
Snooze on the sofa on me till 8:00 am
Play with toy
8:40 am asleep on lap
9:30 am wee
Then in pen with a hoof chew to settle
11:00 am poo and wee
12:00 pm feed and wee
Sleep at Mark's feet, with other dogs loose around her
12:45 pm wee
Feet trim, nail clip and fuss
Potter round with other dogs, supervised
1:20 pm pen to relax
2:20 pm wee
Relax with Mark on the sofa
3:20 pm out for wee and poo

Take pup to horse livery yard, first time in the crate on own in the car, fine. Left her in there to catch Billy in the field (pony) 10-15 minutes left in car and fine/settled/quiet (left her in there mainly to stay warm). Met Billy, and two people at the yard, home 4:30 pm

A visitor came to stay for the night, Alan.
4:35 pm wee in the garden then met Alan.
Feed then sleep in the pen
Out for wee but didn't 6:00 pm
To pub on Alan's lap in car 6:30 pm
Asleep in the soft crate at the pub
7:00 pm wee in the pub garden
Cuddled by two staff at the pub, plus one customer and Alan, calm taking it all in.
Home 8:15 pm wee and feed
Play in pen on own
10:00- 11:15 pm on Mark's lap,
11:45 pm wee and poo
Play on own and with Mark
12:40 am outside but no wee
12:45 am placed in the pen, settled and asleep within 5 minutes.
Out for wee at 3:30 am - we wouldn't usually stay up till this time, but Alan and I were up chatting.

Notes: Settles well in the soft crate, especially with the heat. Likes to sleep when travelling. Poos are now happening regularly so not worried. Likes to watch what's going on. Likes to play tug, working on fetch. Happy to be carried in arms or in the soft crate. Very affectionate and licky.

Having a puppy requires you to have eyes in the back of your head!

When I brought Ripple home - if I couldn't watch her like a hawk she was either on Mark's lap, in her soft crate or in the pen where she is safe. This was for her safety, the other dogs' safety and for housetraining.

I was getting up in the middle of the night, not because she was waking me, in fact, the opposite. I set my alarm to wake me to take her out as she wasn't physically able to hold it all night, this way it helped prevent her learning to toilet in the house (though there was a puppy pad in her crate as an emergency option). It also stopped her screaming waking us up to take her out which then rewards the noise.

Note: I got up in the middle of the night for 11 nights, before she could hold it all night (approximately 7-8 hours).

Don't worry I won't be boring you with every single second of her life, but the first 48 hours may be helpful to start on the right track. It begins from the second they are in your care.

Make sure you have a few days clear for when the pup comes home. Not everything will go to plan, but if you are there you can cope and adapt to what is needed. Keeping calm is crucial. Pups absorb our energy and look to us for guidance. If we are calm and collected it will set them up to be too.

I usually make sure any of my new dogs are not left alone in the house for the first three days, and then start to build up short periods of isolations, 20 minutes, 30 minutes, an hour and so on. By the time they have been home for a week I have usually got to the point where I can confidently leave them for up to two hours in their pen and with no other dogs in sight while we are out of the house. I always leave the puppy with something to do, such as a frozen stuffed Kong, and make sure all their needs are met before going out to ensure they are tired, full and comfortable (not full of beans, a full bladder and hungry).

Collar tips

When you first put a collar on puppy, they will probably scratch at it a lot maybe appear slightly distressed and this is ok. Initially it just feels strange to them; they will settle and forget about it.

You could put the collar on and then distract them with a play session or with a chew or stuffed Kong.

Please do not put it on for the first time and then clip a lead to it and attempt to walk them on the lead straight away. This will cause your puppy to panic.

There are plenty of horror stories about puppies and dogs choking themselves due to their collar and or tag getting caught in crates so please be aware of this and possibly remove it before leaving them alone in a crate.

Little puppies are quick to push through little gaps as doors open so it's worth getting them used to wearing the collar around the house as soon as possible in case they manage to get out of the front door, at least their collar and tag will be on them.

Legally your puppy should always have a collar and ID tag on when in a public place (this is in addition to the microchipping law), this even includes when they are in your vehicle.

This is really useful to get puppy back if they do go missing but from a legal perspective it's for liability purposes.

Did you know that failure to have a collar with correct ID on your dog in public can result in a £5000 fine?!

Even if you only plan to walk your puppy on a harness, they should still wear a collar with ID attached to the collar, not the harness.

You should be able to slide two fingers between pups' neck and collar - though for very small breeds just one finger is sufficient to ensure it fits correctly. They should not be able to pull back out of it. Please remember to check the fit of the collar every few days as they are growing. It's impressive just how fast they grow at this age and we don't want the collar to be too tight around their neck.

What is the correct ID?

Your surname and full address. Not just your house name and postcode. I would always advise putting a mobile number on there too, but this isn't a legal requirement.

Mouthing/biting

The sooner puppy learns that teeth and mouth on you isn't rewarding the better. They have these little needle teeth and they hurt! As soon as they start to put their mouth on you, don't say a word, try to stay calm and remove yourself, step away, all fun and fuss stops for a short while. Get everyone who interacts with puppy to do the same, as soon as they start! Not just when it hurts.

If you are consistent with this you will find that in just a matter of days they stop trying. While this behaviour will likely make a comeback at around 12 weeks it won't be as bad and you will have had a few weeks by then of learning more about each other. See next chapter page 45 for more on mouthing.

Prevent jumping up being an issue in future

Pups love to scrabble up at our legs and when they are cute and tiny we tend to give attention for doing this. We don't have to bend as far and they are adorable and cute and not causing a problem so why wouldn't we? Well this is how jumping up as they are bigger starts, try to only fuss, reward, look, talk and touch them when all four paws are on the floor and ask everyone to do the same so they learn that on the floor is more rewarding. Yes it is cute and adorable when they are so tiny but fully grown with weight and with practice it is not. Never mind the legal implications of dogs jumping up nowadays! See page 225 for more on jumping up.

Tick list for the first week

Get them used to their collar – this chapter
Vet Check See page 33
Building up the time they can be left alone for slowly after the first couple of days.
Crate training See page 127
House training See pages 52 & 123
Bonding/playing with you See page 79
Don't start swapping foods yet if you are changing their diet wait until at least week 2.

Treats and chews See page 91
Preventing jumping up from the start See page 225
Biting/mouthing See pages 43 & 45
Paperwork sorted – registration, microchip, insurance etc.
Signed up to start puppy classes when vaccinations are complete
(or expecting a private trainer to visit this week or next).
Teach them their name and 'watch me' See page 138
Enjoying the cuteness but also how much they sleep too!
Keep a toileting diary to help you predict when they will 'go'.
Caffeine/energy for you as you will be tired from the midnight
alarms.

7 9-12 WEEKS OF AGE

New things to work on:

Sit, down and stand See page 141
Marker word See page 186
Wait See page 144
Leave it See page 147
Stay See page 149
Recall See page 146

Continue to work on:

Positive new experiences
Grooming and handling
Leaving them home alone for short periods
Attention to name
Watch me.
House and crate training

Puppy land shark, mini T-Rex

Those needle sharp teeth hurt, don't they? Puppies explore the world through their mouths, everything gets chewed on, tasted or carried around - including chewing on you initially.

Here is what NOT to do:

Don't squeal, squeak or shout ouch - this will often make it a fun game for many pups and encourage them to do it all the more. This is particularly important with terriers, they were bred to kill small vermin, and if it still is squeaking it's still alive so they must bite and shake harder till the noise stops.

Don't smack or tap your pup to correct them. This can often make the issue worse too.

What to do:

Stop all play, remove your hands, put puppy down if they are in your arms or step away as soon as they put their mouth around you. Don't say a word just remove all fun and interaction.

And/or

Remove yourself and offer an alternative such as a toy or chew for them to express their natural need to chew.

Tip for children - Teach the kids to play statues. Ask them to stand tall, cross their arms and look away from puppy as soon as they start to mouth. This also helps with reducing jumping up too.

There will be times where puppy is adamant, they must chew, they get frustrated and almost appear crazed. The time you are most likely to see this at dusk and dawn and when they are overtired. An overtired puppy can seem like a demon at times, a whirling dervish of teeth and fluff.

You can often start to predict when they may go into this crazed mode. When they go into the wall of death type running around, tail tucked under and off they go for a few minutes. This is called puppy zoomies and is totally natural. It's a puppy's way of expending the excess energy they have and is particularly common when you can't walk them for long periods due to their joints and development.

The zoomies won't cause any harm to them but if they are starting to jump on and off sofas etc. while doing this then we may need to look at other ways for them to expend this energy without such a high risk of injury or knocking household items over in the process.

Once you have noticed the pattern of when it's likely to happen, often called the witching hour too, (most common at dusk and dawn as I said before) just before you think it will happen it's great to do a short training session, just 3 minutes or a play session or give them a filled frozen Kong or long lasting chew in a safe area such as their pen or crate. You could scatter their meal over the garden for them to hunt and find if you are feeding dry food too. All of these things will give them another outlet for their energy, mentally stimulate them and reduce their need to perform the zoomies.

Zoomies can also happen when a puppy has had a busy day! These are the times you may feel deflated, you have done lots with puppy, had a busy day with them and they should just switch off, be tired and give you a little window of peace but instead they are running around like they are the Duracell bunny. Why does this happen? This is often because the puppy is over stimulated; they have done so much they cannot switch off.

If you think about the days when you have been very busy at work, doing lots of different things or rushing around running errands all day, you don't come home till late and although you know you should go straight to bed you know your brain can't switch off yet so you need a couple of hours to wind down, you may even opt to do some extra jobs when you come home as the energy is still flowing... This is the same with puppies and even adult dogs and why you get the zoomies often after those first walks or after a particularly active day, lots of visitors arriving etc. Puppy is very much like the overtired toddler that doesn't want to go to bed on these occasions.

Puppy may not have full on zoomies on every occasion but instead become more vocal, more mouthy or just naughty in general, try not to be deflated or annoyed merely help them learn to relax quicker with a chew or a lickimat or similar.

There will also be times as your pup grows that he may be in low level pain as he grows, just like children they can get growing pains too. This is another factor to consider if it seems your pup is being naughty, chews and enrichment games really are your best friends and path to sanity! See 91 /Chapter 13 Your Secret Weapon.

Puppies need lots and lots of sleep so having a good routine for downtime to give them this chance is great practice. Especially if you have a busy household or have children, puppy will find it hard to switch off and get the rest he needs to be able to process all his learning and grow and mature. Have times each day that they are in their crate or pen or in a quiet, safe room with something to do that isn't high energy to encourage them to switch off.

Lead tips

There are hundreds if not thousands of leads on the market and my best advice is to find one that is soft on your hands, that is around 6ft and has a standard trigger clip.

Please avoid slip/choker, chain leads, extendable or bungee type leads. A standard lead will set you up for success with teaching them how to walk nicely with you as they grow.

If puppy decides to start chewing on the lead, stop and try not to start a game of tug of war. Ask them to sit or distract them with a treat as you then move forward after they have spat the lead out. This phase will pass as long as you are not making it into a game for puppy. You can also use an anti-chew spray such as Grannicks bitter apple spray on the lead to reduce this too.

Having a standard trigger clip is important so it's easy to both clip on and clip off. Puppy will be wriggling at first as you fiddle with a small loop on their collar to attach the lead to and the quicker you can get it on the less you will get frustrated with their wriggling and the less, they will wriggle.

Having a lead that is padded all the way down the lead as well as at the handle will help you to have more patience too. If puppy starts to pull at webbing or new leather or even rope style the lead will hurt your hands. Remember you can hold the lead at any length not just by the handle.

Off lead walks

Your puppy returning to you when off lead is one of the most important things to teach them, it could save their life.

Teaching this also allows you to enjoy more walks and adventures together throughout their life, allowing you both to stay fit and active. This starts at home and in the garden before you can think about doing it out on walks. Starting by playing the round robin recall will really help with this see page 146.

Once I am confident that pup knows their name and will come to me when called around the house and garden I will let them off lead on a walk. This is often very scary for most owners the first time they do it. I will often meet owners of dogs asking for help when their dog is over 12 months of age as they have not had the confidence to try them off lead yet. Please do not leave it this long; the older the dog is when it has not been off lead the harder this is to train reliably.

I will let puppies off lead (again as long as they are responsive to their name at home) before the age of 12 weeks. And there is method in what may seem my madness.

Why let them off lead when so young?

While they are still under 16 weeks of age they are not full of hormones and confidence, they won't wander far away from you because you are their entire world! They rely on you for heat, warmth, food, companionship and safety.

First time letting puppy off lead. What to do and what to avoid.

Find a quiet area, away from roads and distractions such as wildlife other people, and dogs. A field or semi/fully enclosed space. Try and do it when the weather is dry, not frosty and without gusty wind.

Have plenty of tasty treats ready, a poo bag or two and confidence in yourself and your pup!

Walk pup into the field/space, ensure there are no people or dogs coming, in sight or nearby, and clip the lead off their collar. Maybe give them a tasty treat then just walk away.

WHAT?

Yes, just walk away. Try your best not to look at puppy and try not to panic. Keep walking for 20-30 yards and what you will find is puppy is not far behind you. They are insecure at this age and do not want to be left behind. Take a breather and realise you are not going to lose them and that they want to be with you.

I only tend to practice off lead time for short periods, maybe 5-10 minutes for the first few times. But I will practice many things during the time they are off lead.

Things to practice on the first off lead walks

Gently hooking your finger in their collar or harness every time they come back to you and hooking a finger gently before you offer them a treat.

Coming back equals fun, food and fuss – every time.

Sometimes clipping the lead on gently and then clipping it back off so they do not learn that the lead going on signals the end of their freedom.

Sometimes clipping lead on, walking with them on lead for a few yards and then letting them off again.

Crouching down and opening your arms will encourage them to come back to you if they are distracted by a sniff and ignoring you briefly for calling them.

Change your direction of walking regularly, without telling them so they learn to follow you and look to where you are.

Hide behind bushes, trees, gates etc. and wait for them to find you or call them once and wait.

Don't – constantly call them over and over, you become a beacon of noise that they know where you are as they can hear you and can return when they like.

Don't - shout at them if they don't come back fast enough. Who wants to come back to someone who is annoyed and angry when the world/walk is so interesting?

Do – be exciting and encouraging the whole time they are moving toward you. 'Good boy, oh wow who's a clever lad…' etc. to encourage them to continue coming in your direction.

Do – pay or reward them more if they have come from further away or from a distraction.

Don't – always let them off or put them back on lead at the same spot on each walk. They learn quickly and will pull toward or away from these hotspots.

Do – practice this away from other people and dogs for a good while before gradually making it harder by practicing with things in the distance.

Do – start to practice, watch me, sit, down, wait, stay, etc. on walks once you have cracked them at home. Make it easier for them at first, don't ask for much and reward them well.

Remember that they do not need to go off lead every day or on every walk so don't worry if you can't practice this every time you take your puppy out but you should be actively practicing recalls, coming back when called and setting up good habits on every occasion that they are off lead.

Puppy won't toilet on walks?

This is really common while they are still very young and it can cause minor issues with the housetraining process as they come back from a walks and will do their business inside.

Not toileting on walks is all about pup's lack of confidence. By doing their business on walks they are leaving behind lots of information about themselves for other dogs to find. It's a little like people looking at your social media profile and gaining a fair amount of knowledge about you without you knowing. You would shut your privacy down if you were worried and essentially this is what our pups do until they are more confident. Try not to worry too much, it will happen in time and as their confidence grows, just be mindful that if they haven't gone on a walk to take them straight out into the garden to toilet when you return from a walk to ensure you are staying on track with housetraining.

12 weeks old bladders and house training

Keep in mind that most puppies don't have full control over their bladder until they reach 12 weeks of age so accidents will likely happen, even if you have been doing everything you can to speed up the process before this age. Also, even at 12 weeks their bladder is still small and there will be a limit to how long they can hold it for.

Small breeds will have smaller bladders and take a little longer than larger breeds with larger bladders as a very general rule.

Going to new places with your puppy

Of course, we are all excited when we have a new puppy, we want to take it to new places to help socialise them but also to introduce them to friends and family.

The best way to do this is to be prepared, be their advocate and to ensure these are positive new experiences for puppy without getting into bad habits.

What should you take with you?

- Treats! Tasty little morsels to reward them and pay them for being good and doing what you want.
- Poo bags (obvious I know).
- A clean up kit if you are going in the car for any accidents or sickness on route.
- Lead and collar/harness.
- A bed, crate or mat for them to relax on if you are going to a social setting whether in public such as a dog friendly cafe or to a person's house.
- A long lasting chew or filled Kong to help them settle in social settings.

Keep new experiences and environments brief and positive by giving them lots of rewards and words of encouragement and fuss. 15 minutes of something new is ample while they are still under 16 weeks of age.

If they become scared of something or spooked, do not pull them toward it, give them some space and time to decide if they can overcome their fear and be more inquisitive and praise any movement toward the item/object/person. If they are pulling away from it then take them to a distance that they can observe but are more relaxed and not pulling away.

If you have a phobia of spiders, someone pulling you closer to a spider is not going to make you any less fearful, if anything you would become more fearful and start to distrust the person who pulled you closer.

Be your pup's advocate and if something scares them, help them by protecting them and making them feel safer, this is often by moving away. If you can then give them the time and option to make bolder choices, if they don't that's ok too just try again another time.

Depending on where you are going to expose them to new experiences, consider how you would expect them to behave when they are an adult. Do you want a dog who can't keep still in a cafe every time someone moves in expectation of attention from anyone and everyone or do you want a dog who relaxes at your feet oblivious to the rest of the cafe?

Start putting in the basics from the start. Allowing everyone to come and say hi to puppy and make a big fuss of them in the cafe will teach puppy to expect this every time and will really struggle to settle in future.

Instead have your mat or bed and chew ready, ensure they have been to the toilet and are likely to sleep or settle when you get to the cafe and place them on their mat or bed with their chew and calmly verbally praise them for relaxing. You are creating an association in their mind that this is the rules and what is expected in this environment. Yes of course I'm sure other cafe goers and likely the staff will want to talk to and touch puppy but explaining you are training and asking them to ignore puppy would really help make your life so much easier in the future. If puppy gets distracted by the wait staff by the table just encourage them back to their bed and reward them for being there.

Applying this type of thinking to new situations and almost manipulating the environment for your own benefit and setting puppy up for success will speed up the process of training no end.

Plan ahead, guide your puppy and ensure their safety whenever possible.

8 12-16 WEEKS

New things to work on:

Loose lead walking See page 161
Send to bed See page 160
Training them to ask to go out See page 123
Netflix and ~~Chill~~ Crate/crate See page 136

Continue to work on:

Positive new experiences
Grooming and handling
Attention to name
Watch me
House and crate training
Sit, down and stand
Marker word
Wait
Leave it
Stay
Recall

Key reminders for your own sanity:

Paying them for the good stuff not just the bad

Enrichment
Sniff and stroll

You will be at the stage now where it's hard to imagine life without pup but also maybe at that stage where you wondered if you did the right thing if you haven't been there already.

They might be throwing tantrums, chewing things they shouldn't, stealing your dirty underwear to show the neighbours over the fence/in the garden or leaving little smelly presents behind the sofa – or all of it!

Don't panic (Mr Mannering)! We can sort this together and it's all a lot simpler than you may think, plus you are not the only one experiencing this or feeling exhausted by it!

Frustrations and tantrums

Puppy throws a fit when the door shuts and you are the other side, when you try to get their lead on, towel them off or if you try and take them off the sofa for being too excitable. It could be for a number of reasons but this is usually them being vocal, possibly jumping and mouthing too. This is in reaction to them being frustrated at something they want and cannot get. Very similar to a toddler having a tantrum because they don't understand and 'NEED' to have something either they cannot or should not have, and will kick up a fuss in the hope that they get it. Just like with toddlers, this is most likely to happen when they are overtired but can happen at any time of the day.

Dealing with frustration is a key factor in turning your pup into a PupStar. This is a normal part of their development and they simply need guiding through it. Teaching them that all good things come to those who are patient will help you in all areas of your life with your dog. It means that there aren't battles and they have manners that help you both live a fuller life together.

What not to do

Don't 'give in' and give them what they want as a result of them getting frustrated.

Don't get annoyed or shout at them this will often escalate the situation.

Note: this is totally different from the all-out panic that I describe for being let and for crate training etc.

What to do

Teach the wait command and practice it lots – this above anything help will help you more than you think.

Practice that calm quiet behaviour means all the good things happen.

Walk away if you feel you are getting frustrated too and come back to the task once you and puppy are calmer.

Wait it out if you can and it is safe to do so, i.e. wait till they are calm.

Distract them with something else for a moment before returning to it.

If pup is frustrated, and you are struggling and waiting it out till they are calm or distracting them isn't working try asking for something simple like a sit or down or go into the back garden with them for a moment before asking the same again.

Loose lead training – sniff and stroll

While pup is so young and exploring the world I don't put lots of pressure on them for loose lead walking as it's so important that they learn about the big wide world and get to sniff and stroll. At the same time I ensure they are not getting into really bad habits for the future, making loose lead training easier when we start on it more formally.

Tips to make your life easier for the future

Don't take any more steps when they pull ahead, encourage them back, next to your leg (maybe reward them by your leg) before moving on.

Take walks steady, slow and reward often.

Be consistent with which side you expect them to walk on and keep the lead at a length where it can be loose when they are by your side but not long enough that they can cross in front or behind you when they feel like it – the side may change depending on where the traffic is, but you should decide when they change sides not them to ensure they are clear what's expected of them.

Talk to them and encourage them tell them they are wonderful when they are walking nicely.

Don't yank on the lead to get their attention or if they pull ahead.

Naughty children and puppies play up to get told off?

It's easy while puppy is growing for us to slip into the habit of only talking to them to reprimand them when they are doing something they shouldn't. We get tired and forget that they are still learning and so young and expect them just to know that they shouldn't do whatever they are doing. It's easy done, I get it. However the more we go down this particular path the more you will find that pup starts to 'play up'. Why? Because they get attention for it! It may not be good attention but it is attention and a reaction from you all the same. Remember that dogs only continue to do things that they believe pays off in some way; attention from you is exactly that. Just like children who are naughty so they get told off in an attempt at attention.

Try as much as possible to reward anything you see that pup is doing that you like and want more of. Put more importance on this than anything else. It doesn't have to be food rewards every time it could be a good dog, a fuss or a play session.

Stealing items they shouldn't have

This is one of the most common issues I see in young puppies, more so in families who have young children too.

This is what happens ...

Puppy does what they do and puts something in its mouth; they don't know it's not for them or that it might be dangerous. We react and get instantly annoyed, or panic, our body language changes and we go straight toward puppy and pull it out of their mouth.

This only needs to happen a couple of times before puppy recognises the pattern, mainly our reaction and attempts to move away with the item. We often speed up and chase them, maybe shouting no or leave it or drop it. Puppy learns that whatever he has is valuable (because we make them think it is) so it must be kept and also that it's a fun game to run away and be chased. All of this makes us more annoyed and puppy is getting lots of attention.

Puppy soon learns where all the hiding spots are or that they should dispose of the item quickly to avoid you getting it, sometimes this may mean eating said item or it may mean taking it to somewhere out of your reach. Puppy moves faster than us and the more they do it the more we get annoyed and the more they get out of it and so the cycle goes on. See also puppy eating stones if this applies to your puppy page 225.

Easy done, especially with children in the house too!

So how do we start to change it?

We change the association in our pups mind what it means when they have things in their mouth. We teach them that the best place to be when they have something is to be by us!

You need to change your reaction and behaviour too.

Also please avoid pulling things out of pups mouth as this may cause pain as they are teething and encourage them to guard things better the next time as they associate the pulling and your approach with pain.

Using a mixture of the following commands in training and being consistent will help cure this:

- Leave it (if they are approaching said item but it's not in their mouth yet) See page 148
- Give/drop – to spit things out See page 159
- Teaching fetch (and in time carry and find too) See page 193
- Preventing and treating guarding See page 217

Training all of the above and also being consistent with ensuring you are positive with them (which may feel counterintuitive), encouraging them to come to you and fussing them all over their body, not touching their head or the item in their mouth (provided it is an item that is not a danger to their health), even if you have to put on a high pitched voice to talk to them, tell them how amazing they are (fake it if needs be, I get it!). Keep fussing them for what may seem or feel like forever but normally within a couple of minutes they will drop the item naturally. Over time you can practice this method and if you have not got there with the drop/give command this will help. You will start to be able to predict when they will drop the item and say the word just before. The more you do this the less effort it will be and the quicker the dog will drop it. If it's an item that doesn't really matter, sometimes give it back to them or throw it like you would a toy for them, sometimes they lose it altogether too of course but changing things up while they learn is a great thing to do. You can also practice this with toys. Remember to be positive and encouraging, even if you feel like you are rewarding it, I promise this will really help you!

Chewing and mouthing…. AGAIN?!

12 weeks is when the mouthing makes a comeback. You haven't failed or done anything wrong, this is normal as they start to teach and lose their needles at this age. Employ the same tactics as before, ensure they have plenty of cool things to chew on and you may need to use the bitter apple spray again too. Keep calm and carry on. I

promise this will pass again if you are ensuring they have plenty of appropriate things to chew on.

Visitors

Puppy has come home, and family and friends all want to come and meet puppy. They walk in and are all over puppy, saying hi to them cuddling them and playing with them. We are happy with this because we want to see puppy being friendly with different people, its socialisation isn't it? They must meet lots of different types of people and love them, right?

Well yes and no.

Yes, positive associations with new and different types of people are important, but all this excitement at new people coming into the house and the attention on them straight away isn't teaching them how to be calm when people come to the door nor is it teaching them patience.

If you want a puppy that grows into a pain that jumps up and gets overexcited every time Grandma comes over and knocks her over or rips her thin and frail skin with their nails when jumping up, then this is the way to go. It might be acceptable to that friend who loves dogs and says they don't mind and possibly even actively encourages the excitable jumping up but how will Fido know the difference, if sometimes they get rewarded for jumping up and other times, they don't they will keep trying to jump up - it's just the way dogs are.

What's the best way to teach puppy to be calm around visitors?

Have puppy in a separate room or in their crate/pen when you let visitors in the door, have a chat with them and make them a drink and get your visitors settled first. Explain to them that you are starting as you mean to go on with pups training and you would like their help in ensuring puppy doesn't learn bad habits. Ask them to ignore puppy to start with, explain no looking talking or touching for at least 10 minutes/until you say they can. This is hard for visitors as I'm sure it will be for you initially. Cute puppy eyes and little legs scrabbling at you for attention and all that cuteness is really hard to resist.

Release the hound! Have chews and treats to hand. Let them explore, sniff around the new person. Try to keep the new person talking to keep their gaze and focus (again easier said than done with a bundle of cute in front of them). Ask them to ignore any jumping up at them. You can use your voice to encourage them away in a positive tone and reward for coming to you if needed. What we want here is for puppy to investigate, get bored and then settle. If they settle give them a long lasting chew or Kong. Once they have settled for a short while then you can ask your visitor to call the puppy over to interact with them. Remind them about all four paws staying on the floor and if they want to play with them to get on the floor and grab a toy.

Having visitors who aren't that keen on dogs (I'm not suggesting people visit who are fearful of dogs at this point) but people who won't be taken in by cute puppy and will completely ignore them the whole time they are visiting would be great too, so puppy isn't learning that everyone who comes is just there for them.

Eventually (and before you know it) puppy will be bigger, pushier and less cute and people will start to get annoyed if they are jumping up and being rude. When in reality in pups' eyes, they are merely doing what they did when they were younger which was actively encouraged and now, they are getting shouted at for it…. Always consider what patterns routines and habits you are starting right from when they are young.

People on walks

When we have a young pup it's not just visitors to the home that are likely to teach them bad habits if we let them it's also people we see out on walks and outings with our pup. We all do it, 'aw puppy!'

and go and speak to puppy and owner on sight. Most puppies love this but again we have to think about the precedents we are setting for when they are older. It's one thing having people approach and say hello to our pup when they are tiny but when they are twice, or three times the size and dragging you across the road to meet someone who doesn't find them cute and doesn't want to speak to them it's a royal pain in the backside. Not only that but it's dangerous. This can often turn into pup barking and yelling in frustration when they can't meet people because they got to go say hi to everyone when they were younger, and they got lots of attention and praise for it so why is it any different now? Same applies for if we allow them to meet lots of dogs when they are a young baby puppy too.

I also totally get it that the people are not helping for the most part! If you haven't got to this stage yet, it will come! Where you start taking puppy out for those first few walks and you can't get far without being stopped by a well-wishing person wanting to say hi and 'help socialise' your puppy. These are often the times where you will be offered the 'numpty advice' about training your pup so be careful and take it with a pinch of salt.

Best practice when out on walks

When people approach, ask them to 'help you' and ask them to chat to you for a few moments before touching the puppy. While you are chatting to them have those treats to hand and feed puppy, ideally in the sit position. Initially this maybe almost constant feeding while you are telling the stranger/person what their name is, how old they are and explain to them that you are teaching good manners and if puppy jumps up and doesn't have all four paws on the floor when they go to touch and fuss them to step away as soon as they jump. Give permission for the person to say hi and if they fail in their mission (by letting them jump up) take action by calling puppy to you and stepping away from the person so they cannot jump up on them. You can move closer again if you like but the same rules apply each time. This way puppy is not getting to practice the wrong behaviour. Sometimes asking the person to just chat to you and then go on your way without them touching or talking to puppy is brilliant too! Sometimes you may feel rude but consider this. You have to live with this dog, and you want a well behaved and calm companion that you are not embarrassed by every time you go out and pass people or dogs. You are more likely to have more adventures and fun and have a dog who enjoys a varied and rich life when it is well behaved and a pleasure to take places. A dog who isn't well behaved will be left behind more for ease and won't be able to enjoy quite as many experiences by your side.

9 16 – 24 WEEKS/6 MONTHS

Things to work on

Keep up the good work! This is where they will really start to test you! If you feel like they are going backward, take a breather and make it easier for them to get it right. Hormones play havoc with their ability to concentrate.

Work mainly on:

Loose lead walking
Send to bed
Settle
Grooming and handling
Attention to name
Watch me
Wait
Leave it
Stay
Recall

Key reminders for your own sanity:

Paying them for the good stuff not just getting frustrated at the

bad
Patience – take a deep breath
Enrichment and chews will really help

Hormones and puppy license

At 16 weeks you may notice that when pup interacts with other dogs there is a shift in the dynamics. From birth to 16 weeks pups have what is called a puppy license; it means that while they have it they get away with more with older dogs and older dogs will tolerate more rude or inappropriate behaviour from them. At 16 weeks this license gets revoked and other dogs may start to reprimand them for being over excitable, bouncy and rude in dog language. Keep this in mind and reward lots for calm behaviour around other dogs. It's better to manage puppy around other dogs and encourage the right behaviours rather than let the dogs 'sort it out' as this can often end in a negative association with other dogs.

Why does this happen at 16 weeks? Because this is when their hormones start to develop and other dogs can smell this on your puppy. It's a little like the fact that we will tolerate more from a young child but when they become a teenager we start to be stricter with the rules and boundaries because they are now old enough to understand and it's also natural for them to push these boundaries due to their hormones.

Many owners may not notice a stark difference in their hormonal and testing behaviour till they are 5-6 months of age but this is where it starts building from.

There will be a surge in energy levels and less sleep for puppy now and this may be the biggest difference to you. You may feel the need to take them out for longer walks to try and tire them out. It's also tempting to let them play with other dogs on walks regularly as that tires them out too and gives you some peace so you can get on with work or get the chores done.

Walking them for longer and longer is not advisable. I speak more about the health and physical development side in chapter 12 on exercise but if nothing else consider that the longer you walk them the fitter they are getting, by doing this you are essentially training an athlete and they will just crave more and more the higher their fitness level gets and it's hard to keep up with that!

The best way to help them and give yourself a break without making them into an Olympic athlete is by doing lots of enrichment activities, chews and brain games (see chapter 19 Hacks and Enrichment page 205). Short training sessions too, when I say short I mean 3 minute sessions, even if it's not training something you have been working on, training a trick or training them to chill and be still are great ways to tire their brains out.

Try to remember that they are still very young, they are learning so much all the time and they are struggling with their changing bodies and brains. Some compassion and understanding goes a long way.

Remind yourself of all the issues you have overcome together, the many things you have trained and the times you have had together. The cute adorable fluffball that you get to cuddle up with, yes there is nothing cuter than a sleeping pupster, and it makes us feel warm and fuzzy when they chose to do that on or by us. Focus on these things when you find yourself getting frustrated or defeated. There is light at the end of the tunnel I promise!

Socialising your puppy with other dogs

We do want our dogs to be confident around other dogs; we don't want them to see them as a threat either. It's really important to find a balance between the two and know what to look for when dogs do meet.

How to ensure your dog doesn't listen to you around other dogs!

A fool proof recipe for a nightmare dog…

Take your dog, let them play and interact with every dog it sees, let them have the best fun with other dogs regularly. Let them chase and pull to get to their buddies on every walk. Better still, ensure you go looking for other dogs when out walking your dog, just so your dog can have a good tear around and come home tired. You could go one better and get another dog and let them play with each other all of the time. Congratulations you have just created a nightmare of a dog.

You have created the dog that will not listen to you call when other dogs are around, the dog who will run at full pelt when it sees a dog miles away, oblivious to your calls, shouts and screams for them to come back. You have created a dog that will do absolutely anything to be with other dogs rather than you. Who will pull your arm out and drag you towards dogs on the street? A dog with enough practice will bark and lunge and snarl at other dogs when on lead as they cannot contain their frustration at not being able to play with their buddies. They will look and sound like the hell hound causing you much embarrassment and frustration.

No really this is exactly what happens, and I am a true believer in dogs only meeting maybe one in ten dogs they see if not much less. Particularly when they are on lead.

It's a little like us going to Tesco and saying hi and having a conversation with every single person we see. Imagine it 'Hi, my name's Sarah, those are lovely potatoes you are weighing there.' 'Hi, my name's Sarah, I like apples too'... 'Hi'...you get the picture. It would be weird, and I would get a lot of very strange and unwelcoming looks!

From a health and development perspective play can cause real damage to your puppy's growing form. An injury is so easy at a young age as their skeleton is so soft, almost like jelly. Differences in size and weight between puppy and adult dog needs to be a real factor for consideration here.

Humans playing with dogs with toys and food? Yes, yes, yes! Don't forget it's so important that we bond with our dogs more than they bond with each other.

Letting them play with each other? Hmm, not a great idea on the whole.

Dogs speak dog. Well duh of course they do but this means we have to convince them that we are more fun than them speaking dog to other dogs!

Honestly, it's not something I encourage. When in fact all we have to do is become the fun factor! Toys, treats, find it, games and training.

If you have already inadvertently followed the recipe above, all is not lost you can turn your nightmare pooch into a pleasurable one, with some work and plenty of fun for both of you. It's a matter of knowing how and learning what your dog loves and using it.

What is the right way to socialise your pup with other dogs?

More importance should be put on passing dogs on walks calmly. The pup does not get to meet every dog it sees, and it gets a reward for coming past dogs or seeing dogs at a distance and not pulling toward them. A reward can be a fuss, treat or a play session in this instance, depending on what's appropriate/easiest for you at the time. Try not to only rely on a stroke or fuss as a reward for this as it will not be enough 'wages/payment' to pup in some instances and will lead to them eventually becoming the frustrated greeter. For example - the dog at a distance, puppy responds to you calling its name easily = fuss/good dog. Dog a little closer, pup responds to you or ignores dog completely = treat or play. Dogs are all about distance…the closer something is, the harder it is to ignore…so pay your pup accordingly.

Also, it's worth remembering that there will be instances your pup cannot possibly listen or respond to you… this is usually because the other dog is simply too close and too interesting. In these instances, stay calm and relaxed and simply move pup further away to a distance where it can respond to you and be rewarded. Try not to keep calling pup's name, talking or shouting at it when it is in the frenzied state of wanting to get to the other dog, your energy is being fed to pup and it will react in a negative way to this (i.e. I would definitely rather be with my own kind right now than with this unstable, frustrated, angry human). Not only that but the more times you call pup's name, and it ignores you the more it learns that ignoring you is an option, and it can be repeated next time. Just move away with the puppy, staying quiet and reward when the pup is more relaxed and can respond.

If you have friends with older role model type, calm dogs, arrange to go on a short walk with them and their dog. Don't bring the dogs close enough to meet initially, keep them on lead and walk parallel with enough space between you so the dogs don't get to sniff each other yet.

Puppy will likely get a little frustrated on lead at this point but just encourage them verbally to walk and come with you. Ignore any whinging, barking or whining at the point. This will get less after just a few hundred yards. If either dog stops go to the toilet let that dog move away after and then take the other to sniff the spot - this may sound strange, but this allows each dog to learn more about each other, gain lots of information without stress and will really help them. It's the equivalent of checking someone out on social media or checking their 'Peemails'. As you progress gradually bring the dogs closer together while walking parallel, if puppy starts to pull away from the other dog or pull toward in an excited manner then just allow a little space again and try again when they are calmer.

Parallel walking is the safest way to introduce dogs, but this won't always be possible.

There will be times throughout your pup's lifetime that you walk around a corner in the street and suddenly there is another dog in your pup's face, likely when both are on lead.

Many adult dogs are not happy to meet other dogs when they are on lead but are more than happy to when they are off lead. Why is this? Because when they are on lead, they do not have the option to run away or get more space so they feel insecure and will often lash out because that's what makes them feel safer - a case of I'm going to get you before you get me and that's what keeps me safe. We don't want your puppy to learn how to do this so let's have a look at how to deal with these situations.

The 5 second rule when meeting dogs on lead

Unless the other dog has approached growling, barking or with very stiff body language (more on this soon) then it's very unlikely that within 5 seconds and provided you follow the rules that something will go wrong.

Dogs would naturally approach each other in a C curve and end up nose to the other dogs bum so try to allow or create this shape where possible.

Keep your lead loose! This will be hard at first as you may be nervous but by putting tension on the lead you may be causing the puppy to show the wrong body language to the other dog. You may need to almost walk into the dogs, closer to allow a loose lead.

You may need to circle around to keep the lead loose and ensure the leads don't get tangled pulling their faces together.

Talk in a calm but reassuring voice, telling them how great they are.

Count to 5 in your head before calling pups name and taking a few steps away from the other dog and encouraging pup to come with you and reward for coming away. This is also a great starter point for calling away from other dogs when off lead too.

It's great practice to then ask for a sit or to focus on you while you chat to the other owner briefly (without the dogs interacting) before continuing your walk.

Don't forget they should be learning that you are more fun to be around than other dogs and walking past and ignoring dogs is the norm and they only get to meet the occasional dog with your permission.

10 6-12 MONTHS

This is often the hardest stage and the age where many owners will give up, you won't though – we have got this!

Work mainly on:

Management See page 95
Loose lead walking
Send to bed
Settle
Grooming and handling
Attention to name
Watch me
Wait
Leave it
Stay
Recall

Key reminders for your own sanity:

Paying them for the good stuff not just getting frustrated at the bad
Patience – take a deep breath
If you can't train it, manage it!

Make it easier for them to get it right
Enrichment and chews will really help

Often the owners of pups will have been led to believe around the age of 6-8 months is the best time to have their puppy neutered or spayed. Or they get frustrated with the hormone-fuelled behaviour particularly in male dogs and get them 'fixed' with the belief not only is it the best thing for their dog but it is also likely to make the annoying behaviours lessen or stop completely. Unfortunately, this is rarely the case. I am not anti-spay/neuter, nor am I pro. My own experiences both professionally and from what my dogs tell me (aside from the complicated considerations for a multi-dog household) that having them 'fixed' at this age, lessens their ability to grow up mentally. We wouldn't do it to a teenage boy or girl so why would we do it to a dog? Neutering early (i.e. before the body has fully grown and matured) in male dogs is proven to make them grow taller and can cause bone and joint issues in the future. With female dogs, you are removing the hormones that keep them calm, and while in both sexes it takes 12 weeks for the hormones to dissipate totally, and usually people see an improvement during this period. The issues that they had hoped to fix usually return after this period of adjustment. Now this isn't the case for all, and yes there are benefits to spay and neuter for which I'm sure you have heard from your vet. But if you can wait just another 6-12 months it will make little to no difference to their chances of cancer, and you will end up with a more rounded, mature adult dog at the end of it. Do some research, particularly for your breed (or the mix of breeds if applicable). Each breed is different, and most breed clubs will have guidelines and advice sheets on this subject. The Dachshund breed council are now recommending if and only if you would like to get your dog spayed or neutered it's best to do it once they are over 2 years (considering this is a small, fast maturing breed, it wasn't what I was expecting). Neutering younger can increase their chances of back problems.
In some breeds such as the Golden Retriever and Rottweiler it has been found that neutering male dogs is detrimental and is likely to cause osteoporosis. Every dog is different, and every breed is different, and also your mix of dogs, so a lot to consider here.

It's worth remembering with male dogs once their hormones have peaked, things start to get easier, it's not going to be like that forever! Just sit tight, keep calm and breathe!

Female dogs often calm down in their behaviour after their first season, but then start to push boundaries, almost become manipulative in a very sneaky, subtle way - again sit tight and keep calm, it will get easier.

Hormones will peak and you may be tempted to just give in and 'get them fixed', please try to hang in there, I promise you it gets better, this phase passes and life gets so much easier!

Hormonal behaviour isn't just about humping, marking and looking for mates. Hormones are helping their development both physically and mentally and you may not see any of these 'issues'.

They will struggle to concentrate, they will appear to forget all of their training and they will get frustrated more and appear to play up more every time you get annoyed.

It's worth keeping in mind that dogs can hear our heart rate. So even if we haven't said anything or even moved, the second we start to get annoyed our heart rate changes and they will pick up on this, take a deep breath, count to ten, leave the room if need be till you are calmer.

Secondary fear period

This is something which you may notice or you may not, but it's certainly worth keeping an eye out for. For large breeds such as German Shepherds, this is usually around 7 months of age, younger for smaller breeds and older for larger. This is a period in which your dog may 'spook' or become fearful of sights and sounds that they have previously been okay with. This usually passes fairly quickly. Sometimes after a couple of days in other cases, it can be 2-3 weeks. During this time it's important that your pup isn't exposed to things that could make him very fearful. The odd spook is fine but if they have a bad experience such as a dog attacking them during this time it is something that will stay with them for months and often years ahead. This stage is normal as part of your pup's development. You may find they become a little barkier at general things during this period, in which case it's essential to manage the amount that they can practice barking at things that can trigger this behaviour during this period.

7-11 months is the hardest stage of having a pup. Pup will be pushy, have little to no concentration, have days where it will feign deafness, and you will question whether you did ever teach them to sit, wait, or anything for that matter. Training wise...more patience needed. Yes, even more than before. Back to basics with training and making everything as easy as possible for them. For example, if they could previously do a one minute stay and now can barely do 30 seconds, just ask for 20 seconds for a few repetitions before gradually building up to a minute in small increments. Don't be stingy or tight with your rewards, pay your dog well and he will want to repeat it and even try harder the next time!

Recall or coming when called when off lead usually starts to be affected during this stage, go somewhere else, hide from your dog, make it fun, take better smellier treats for coming back, don't let them have as much off lead exercise as before so you can concentrate on increasing their response to the recall command while they are off lead.

Neural pruning

This happens around 10-12 months for small to medium dogs and 12-18 months for large breeds, 18-24 months for giant breeds.

It's your pup's brain filtering out what is important information and what's not, linked to this is the secondary fear period as described above. Just like your computer doing a defrag, or emptying the trash folder. It's your pups brain deciding what or who is safe and reliable in its world, what behaviours 'pay' (this can be a self-reward such as stealing food off the side or that they feel good when they chase or play with other dogs or it can be sitting and waiting for his food gets him a big reward - his meal at the end of it) and what behaviours don't pay.

If you have ignored jumping up on you and not given eye contact, verbal commands or touched them (which can all be perceived as rewards) consistently, your dog will deem this behaviour as a waste of energy and cease to repeat it. This doesn't mean once they have their first birthday they can do what they like, but it does mean you can begin to relax things and move forward.

Management is your best friend for all things dog training but more so at this age than any other. It will keep your sanity and also ensure pupster isn't getting to practice the bad habits so you can return to training when you can and when they can concentrate a bit more.

11 PLAY WITH YOUR DOG

Play Tug!

I often get asked about this subject, and there is lots of conflicting advice out there about it on Google!

Will playing tug teach my dog to be aggressive or to guard things?
If played correctly, no! If anything, it should help with these issues.

Will playing tug stop my dog from giving the ball or toy back
when playing fetch?
If played in the right way, no not at all.

So how should we play tug?

Before anything else you need to have or teach a reliable release or drop/give command this is as important as the game itself. If you have a large breed it's unlikely that you will be able to physically win the game without this as their grip is too strong and their weight and bite pressure is working against you.

The golden rules for playing tug in the right way

You must let the dog 'win' the item often (we let go and let them have the toy for a short while). If we don't let them 'win' it simply becomes boring to the dog, there is nothing to gain from play, so they stop even trying to grab the item in the first place.

You must 'win' often too, slightly more than you let the dog win (maybe 60% of the time), remembering to win the last time of the session before putting the toy away, only to be given to the dog during the next game.

The toy ideally should be a toy that is kept out of reach of the dog and is kept especially for playing tug, this helps to keep the dog's interest and is a 'prize to be won'. Toys that are around all the time for the dog are of less interest (though still useful to have around for the dog) and as such will be of less value to the dog.

Keep your motion when playing tug low and pull the toy side to side rather than up and down. Up and down motions can harm a dog, pulling muscles and put a lot of strain on the shoulders and forelimbs with each bounce.

Make the toy move like prey would, stop and start the movement, make it zig and zag, slow and fast on the ground to get their interest to chase and grab it.

Keep sessions short (2-3 minutes) and fun!

If the dog is struggling to give up the toy when asked (so you can win) do not carry on moving, keep hold of the toy and go very still, this is a clear cue to the dog that the fun stops when they don't listen/respond. Give a verbal reward such as good dog when they release the toy.

Tug can be a fantastic tool to use in place of treats as a reward and can be used to teach impulse control.

It's always worth being mindful of your dog's age too, if they are 6 months or under they could still be teething and this game may make their mouth sore, so go gentle and don't worry if they go through a phase of not wanting to play, come back to it in a week or two and try again. My own dog, Ripple went through a phase at around 6 months of not wanting to tug; it lasted about a fortnight before she was 'into it' again.

If you are playing with an older dog, if they are usually very enthusiastic about playing tug and suddenly are not, it may be worth getting their teeth checked at the vet.

Tug toys also have another potential use - you can soak them in water from your dog's food if you soak it or dog gravy, or doggy yoghurt etc. you can soak it in something tasty and freeze it. Giving it to your dog frozen to lick and chew (under close supervision so they do not destroy or swallow the toy) is something you may want to try.

Notes about playing fetch and tug while puppy is still small

Puppy necks are really delicate, they're still developing. Hold toys low and allow the puppy to pull rather than you tugging.

Fetch is a very repetitive game you need to do this just a couple of times each session, rather than keep doing it till they get bored. Repetitive movements are not good. It's more about variety being the spice of life.

Play Fetch

You will find specific instructions on how to train this in a different way in chapter 18 page 197 (fetch carry and find) if this doesn't work for you.

The fetch toy ideally should be a toy that is kept out of reach of the dog and is kept especially for playing with you; this helps to keep the dog's interest and desire to play with you and the toy. Toys that are around all the time for the dog are of less interest (though still useful to have around for the dog) and as such will be of less value to the dog.

Initially with a small pup the easiest way to teach this is to get puppy interested in it and then toss the toy just a few yards away from you, they will likely run toward it and if they pick it up naturally use your voice in a high pitched manner and encourage them back to you, lots of fuss and praise when they do come back to you and then fuss them all over their body, don't go straight for the toy, don't touch their head yet.

Keep fussing them for what may seem or feel like forever but normally within a couple of minutes they will drop the item naturally. With practice you will start to be able to predict when they will drop the item and say the word just before. The more you do this the less effort it will be and the quicker the dog will drop it. When they drop the toy, praise them and throw it again. Try to only do this two to three times before doing something else each time you are practicing and training this initially. By just doing it a few times and then putting the toy away you will keep up their desire to want to do it again and not get bored and wander off. Over time you can build up the amount of repetitions but it is best not to overdo it so they get bored.

Key things to remember

Be encouraging and excited when they pick up the item. I don't use treats for this method of training. Praise, fuss and the toy being thrown again are often enough

Don't reach or go to touch the toy or their head at this stage as they will start to shy away and possibly run off with it expecting to be chased.

Pups and dogs that go to lay down with an item are more likely to chew and destroy it so calling them over to you before they lay down is a great way to keep the toys in good condition to be able to make them last longer.

Troubleshooting

If pup keeps running off to their bed or favourite spot with the toy rather than coming back to you, you can try either of the following things; once you have tossed the toy for them to fetch move toward the area they will take it, often their bed or comfy spot.

Consider the value of the toy, if it's new or too valuable to the puppy they are less likely to want to share it with you and want to take it away to chew it so maybe try with a less exciting toy to start with.

You can also try the swap it game, by having two identical toys, but ensure they bring it all the way back to you and drop it before you throw the second – this is particularly helpful if your dog has learnt to guard the toy a little. See chapter 20 page 221 for more guarding tips and solutions

Words of warning

Using treats at this stage for fetch is often counterproductive and puppy learns to drop the toy a few yards from you, come and get the treat then return to the toy before you can get it or they just learn to not bring it all the way back to you.

Don't throw the ball too far; this can result in puppy losing interest in it.

Don't make your pup an adrenaline junkie by playing fetch lots and lots, even if they adore the game it's not good for their mental and physical wellbeing

Take them on a walk and blast the ball for a bit to tire them out?

Please, please do not do this. The repetition of chasing, stopping and twisting to come back to you can and will cause unnecessary strain on their joints and ligaments.

Also consider that every time they get to chase a ball or toy and you have put no control training with it they are just learning and practicing how to chase things that move, this skill is often transferred to chasing small furries, wildlife or in some cases bicycles, runners etc. too.

Ball flingers are not good!

The plastic sticks that you put a ball on the end of and it gives you the ability to throw them further and also saves your back from bending over to pick it up? Yeah, don't do it.

It's a failsafe way to create an adrenaline junkie if your pup loves to play fetch. It's also a great way to cause injury and strain.

I love to teach pups how to play fetch and will start to use the desire for the toy more than treats over time as a reward or to get and hold their attention in very distracting environments. I also like to teach them to find the toy and return when I have hidden it so they can give their brain a work out using their nose which tires them in a healthier and calm way.

Breed specific notes

Terriers are more excited by the chase of the moving object than the returning it so lots of praise and encouragement needed for picking it up and returning to you with it in their mouth.

Herding breeds, primarily collies/sheepdogs – if they have missed the movement of the ball/toy i.e. they were not looking when you threw it they will struggle to find it as they are very visual movement aware but not so great at noticing static objects visually.

12 EXERCISE & WALKS

Exercising a puppy shaped jelly

Exercise for your pup - how much is too much? Often less than you think.

The very general rule and probably the easiest to remember is 'the 5 minute rule.'

Only walk your pup for 5 minutes for each month of life. For example, a 6 month old puppy should only be having 30 minutes exercise (5 minutes x 6 months = 30 minutes). This should be for all breeds up to Labrador size up until 12 months of age, and for larger breeds such as Newfoundland's, Great Danes, St Bernard's, etc. up to 2 years of age.

The 5 minute rule is great; an even better guide to work from is the Puppy Culture puppy exercise guide which you can buy online or view on Google images. It's very specific with types of exercise and size of dog and age of the dog.

Why? Because puppy's bones and joints are still developing, they are very soft and can easily be damaged.

The biggest part of the exercise for a young puppy should be in free play that means exploring and just generally mooching around

If puppy decides that they're tired and they just flop down or refuse to walk you need to make sure that you listen to them, the worst thing you can do is go on lots of repetitive style walks so whether that's a march for long distances around the pavements or a big hike, that kind of exercise is going to lead to future joint and physical development issues.

Something to be really mindful of is how much your puppy is jumping off things, jumping up things and going up and down the stairs. All of these things can really increase their risk of a spiral fracture or any future issues, so reduce this as much as possible. Stair gates are always a good idea with a young puppy.

No running with your puppy under 12 months at all. Puppy can choose to run of his own accord but you should not go running, cycling or jogging with them.

8 to 16 week old puppies

No more than 200 feet at a time walking in a straight line as if you're going for a normal walk, break up any amount of this kind of walking with stopping and sniffing maybe a little bit of training. Formal loose lead walking training should be limited to 2 minutes.

Jumping, landing and high impact activities should be kept to an absolute minimum and we should manage their opportunities to be able to do this.

They can swim at this age if they choose to but they should never be forced. Consider purchasing the lifejacket and ensuring that they're not going in deep water as they will tire very quickly, we don't want them to panic.

4-6 months

400 yards of sustained walking, (i.e. walking in a straight line on lead on pavements for example).

Up to 45 minutes of sniff and stroll at a slow pace on soft ground, at puppies pace at 6 months of age.

6-12 months

Build up to 20-30 minutes of sustained walking at 12 months of age. But they can do up to an hour sniff and stroll, slow and with breaks and stops. The key is to listen to puppy if they stop or get tired.

I have done it all wrong before, with Ziggy my miniature Dachshund when he was a tiny pup. I took him out with my bigger, older dog Bella every day for an hour. Bella would chase a ball back and forth for the whole of the walk, and Ziggy would chase behind her. I did this from a young age (maybe 4/5 months old), and I remember taking him to the vet for something routine at around 8 or 9 months old and saying to the vet, 'I'm sure I'm over exercising this pup' (I was not working with dogs professionally then, and knew very little, other than I wanted the very best for my dogs and had limited knowledge). The vet responded with something like, 'oh he's a small dog, he will let you know when he's had enough, don't worry about it'. At age 18 months Ziggy was diagnosed with arthritic hips, and this was due to my naivety of over exercising him while he was still growing and maturing.

Ziggy isn't, never has and never will be the type of dog who will let me know when he's 'had enough' he would go all day if I let him, he's still a bouncy, happy chap at 15 years of age but when he does 'overdo it' he is stiff that evening or the next day. The 5 minute rule is becoming more and more common knowledge, which is great, but there is still the misconception that it only applies to big dogs. It refers to all sizes, as Ziggy and many others have proven.

Think about it in human terms. You would not ask a 5 year old child to walk for 10 miles, would you? Nor would you ask a 10 year old child to carry a heavy load.

Other things to consider while the pup is still growing are things like how often they are jumping off furniture, if you are allowing them to jump in and out of vehicles, playing with other dogs and going up and down stairs. All of these things have an impact on their joints and should be kept to an absolute minimum while young to ensure long-lasting health in their adult life.

During this phase, there is nothing wrong with occasionally meeting up with friends and their adult dogs (provided that they are good role models for the pup of course) and going for a short stroll or meeting at a cafe or pub or going around to their house for a catch-up. This teaches the puppy that other dogs are ok too but putting a lot of importance on not doing this where the other dog is still young and very playful.

In dog agility you are not allowed to compete with your dog until they are 18 months of age, this is due to the wear and tear on their bodies when jumping/landing, twisting and turning through weaves and doing a tight turn to the next piece of equipment. In most other dog sports, there is a minimum age limit to compete and another to move up a level too. Again, due to their bodies maturing, and to help prevent damage.

While some of the above will only apply to when you get puppy home it's worth considering some these things now. No matter what breed or size of dog you are hoping to join your family all of the above needs to be considered and planned for in advance. I guarantee you as soon as you mention to your other dog owning friends that you are planning to get a pup, they will be at the very least thinking about how you can get your puppy 'socialised with theirs' and more than likely suggesting times dates and places you can go and meet up to ensure your puppy is 'socialised properly' because 'it worked for their dog' it may have been ok for their dog, but it may not for yours. Set the boundaries now. Blame it on me! 'Sarah said we shouldn't do X because of Y and I plan to stick to it…Sorry!'

Easy clean/slippy flooring

Ceramic or stone tiles, laminate flooring, linoleum and polished wooden flooring all pose a risk to your pup's health if not managed

Having floors that are slippy are not good for a growing puppy, nor an adult dog.

Although great for cleaning up accidents and maybe cute to watch your pup slide around as they take a corner too fast etc. it's not good for their skeletal development nor their confidence. Consider whether you need to by some cheap nonslip mats to help your pup get around. I say cheap due to risk of chewing and if pup has an accident on them. Ideally some that are small enough for you to put in the washer from time to time but also heavy enough that your pup does not get into the habit of pulling them around everywhere.

Accidents, strains and injuries are very easy when they are so young and just putting somethings in place to avoid this for something that is easily avoidable is certainly worth thinking about and acting on.

An alternative option would be to regularly put paw wax on your pups paws each day, so they have more grip, and you don't have to worry about mats and extra rugs etc.

13 YOUR SECRET WEAPON

Chews - Such an undervalued tool!

Dogs need to chew, adults as well as puppies!

Kongs are, in my opinion THE best invention to keep dogs occupied, ever!

They are a rubber toy that has a hole through the middle that you can stuff with treats etc. You can also use these for play too as their shape means they bounce from the ground erratically which is exciting and keeps the interest of many dogs.

Kong stuffing is a great way to keep your pups or adult dog occupied and tired. Filling these with treats, their daily food, soft cheese, meat paste, banana etc. and then placing in the freezer.

Giving frozen, stuffed Kongs to puppies and adult dogs makes the challenge harder, for it involves lots of licking and chewing to get at the tasty treats inside. This not only reduced mess but it also helps to sooth teething gums. I have included a Kong stuffing ideas and guide in your free bonuses which you can get here – www.multidogmaven.co.uk/pupstarbonus

Please do not feed your dog Rawhide!

Rawhide is bad, really bad.

With ingredients such as leather, glue and dog… yes really – you are making your dog be a cannibal! I'm sure that won't sit well with you, it certainly doesn't me!

Not only are the ingredients disgusting, but these products are harmful to your dog - they are unable to digest them and eventually you are likely going to end up with a very poorly dog and a big bill at the vets due to a blockage.

Please do not buy Roasted Knuckle Bones for your dog

I used to work in pet shops and would often bring home chews and toys for my dogs for when I was out at work (and if I'm really honest it was because I felt guilty about leaving them for so long). I often brought home the roast knuckle bones for my guys as they loved them, and they would last for so long. When one of my own dogs, Jazz was around a year of age I woke one morning, ready to get the dogs ready for an early walk before I headed off for a long day at work, I came into the kitchen to see my beautiful girl in her crate and sat in a pool of her own blood. Not a nice sight to wake up to or see at any time. She was lethargic and after I checked her over, I could see the blood was coming from her back end. We rushed straight off to the vets, where she stayed for the day. I hated leaving her there and was so worried about her; I also had thoughts and fear of potentially losing her in my mind. She spent the day at the vets, I was on the phone to them every hour to see what was going on and if she was ok. She had had X-rays and they had shown a shard of cooked bone had ripped her intestines as it was trying to pass through. An operation to remove the offending item and also the sew up her intestines followed and luckily my girl came home to me safe. A large vet bill, and some careful recovery protocols to go through along with painkillers, anti-inflammatory medications and strict instructions to not feed cooked bones again. I had more than learnt my lesson. These are a real danger to your dog's life; these bones were around the same size as her and yes, she still managed to break a piece off and ingest it.

Dogs cannot digest cooked bones. Best case, they will pass shards of it without issue, some will stay sat in the gut for years if not indefinitely and worst case they can cause death from internal bleeding or causing immovable blockages, please do not ever give your dogs any kind of cooked bone. Even if they are in pet shops this is no guarantee of safety! If you are buying bones from the pet shop and it's not stored in the freezer it is cooked - don't waste your money and put your dog's life at risk.

So, what is best to use if not rawhide or knuckle bones?

Long lasting chews

Bulls Pizzles
Beef hide
Hooves (non-filled ones, though you can fill them if you wish. The ones that come filled from the pet shop are full of grit).
Yak chews
Tendons
Pigs ears (fatty but ok if your dog isn't on a diet or having lots of them)

Longer lasting chews

These are less interesting/less valuable - however more hygienic to leave around the house and are great for your dog to chew on if they suddenly feel the need to chew.

Stag antlers
Buffalo horns
Root chews

Having a mixture of both of the above is the best practice. Longer lasting available to them most if not all of the time around the house and the other type kept for when you need them.

Chewing is normal for dogs and they need an outlet for this otherwise they start to chew things we don't want them to like our furniture or shoes etc. It's not just puppies who need to chew.

Chewing is a stress reliever, it's mentally stimulating making the dog or puppy tired and it's also a pain reliever. Providing our dogs with things to chew throughout their lifetime is very beneficial just as much for us as it is for them.

Other common chews that are best to avoid

This is due to less than desirable ingredients or the dog's inability to digest them:

Popular brand dental sticks
Coloured munchy rolls
Roast knuckle bones
Bones you have cooked (leftover from a roast maybe)
Any cooked bones

14 MANAGEMENT

'Practice makes perfect, but who thinks it's perfect? You or the dog?'

Management is about manipulating the environment/situation and protecting the puppy from being able to practice the wrong things. Management is not training, but it is an extremely useful tool. In some cases a management solution to a dog not coming back off lead would be to keep the dog on lead or if a dog is reactive or barking at other dogs the management solution would be to avoid other dogs.

While none of these solutions are 'curing' the dog of the issue, it is preventing the dog from practicing the wrong behaviour. This provides a window of opportunity to work on replacing the unwanted behaviour with a new and desirable behaviour as and when you can control the environment and set the dog up for success. Without management as part of any training plan, you will fail.

Just like us if we want to break a bad habit it isn't productive to go back to the old habit between practicing the new habit. For example let's look at smoking, when a person quits smoking they try to replace the time that they would smoke with something else. This may be having a mint, or distracting themselves in some other way while the cravings are at the forefront of their mind. If they sometimes had a cigarette and sometimes didn't, you wouldn't consider them to be an 'ex-smoker' would you? A dog who has practiced a behaviour just a handful of times is a lot easier to train to do an alternative behaviour, than a dog who has had years and years of practising the wrong thing on what could be a daily basis. Patience is key, remember that training takes time and management solutions will help you in your journey to success.

Easy management solutions for puppies

Problem - puppy is toileting on the best rug in the front room
Management – remove rug or stop allowing puppy in the room when not actively being watched
Training plan – only allow puppy on rug when watched or you are playing with them or training them. Continue work on housetraining in general

Problem – pulling on lead
Management – only walk them off lead in safe areas to exercise
Training plan – only put them on lead when you can train them and you are prepared

Problem – getting over excitable with visitors to the house
Management – shutting dog in another room or in crate when visitors come or having dog on a lead when you answer the door preventing them from jumping all over them
Training plan – work on calm greetings, response to the doorbell and practice with willing friends with lead on to start with

Problem – stealing things they shouldn't and running of
Management – removing anything that could be stolen or preventing their access in someway
Training plan – work on drop/give, fetch, and leave it. Change their association and your reaction to the thefts.

15 SPEAK DOG

Dog speak all the time. I'm not talking about barking but they are constantly giving signals as to their feelings and emotions. Not just by using their tail either. If we can learn to listen/read them the easier life will be with them.

A wagging tail isn't always a happy one

A dog's tail wagging doesn't necessarily mean that they're happy.

If it's very upright and very short, stiff wags. That can be high alert, and that can then progress into aggression or grumbling, being vocal, but not what we want. They're all signs to say they're not happy.

If its short stiff wags but low and almost between their legs this means they are unsure, scared and insecure.

Loose, big rhythmic wags that are mid-level - neither very high nor very low is a sign of a happy dog.

Again, this is breed-depending. This is very good for, say, if you've got a Labrador or a German Shepherd, but if you've got something like a Tibetan Terrier, for example, they have a very upright curly tail, so it's a lot harder to read this. They all have a different relaxed tail placement.

With a curly tail - they will hold it in different ways and move it in different ways. It's about learning to translate this to that type of dog.

The shake-off

Dogs will do a whole-body shake. Like if they get out of the river or out of the bath, for example, they'll do the whole-body shake to shake the water off. We all know what that looks like, but dogs will do this quite regularly anyway throughout the day, even when they're not wet. Now, what this is called is an adrenalin shake-off, and it basically means they've got so excited or so anxious about something, depending on what's going on, that they know that they absolutely stink of adrenalin, at least to other dogs, and they shake it off, and it calms them down.

It's a bit like if we're in a stressful meeting, for example with work, and then you walk out the door, you shut the door and you have to take a big sigh, like 'Hooo,' and that's you calming yourself down and you're kind of like, 'Right, okay. Yeah. Okay, I can go back in now.' The shake-off is the same in the dogs. Start to take a mental note of when they're doing this. It's quite common that when you go to put the lead on, and then they shake off as you're about to leave for the walk, or as you're locking the door as you're leaving for the walk, or after a big play session that you've had with them.

Again, it can be excitement, but it can be adrenalin because they're worried or anxious. I always tell my guys, and I'm always telling clients, that when they shake off, I always go, 'Good dog,' because I like to acknowledge it. That makes me take a mental note of what's just gone on beforehand. What's made them do that? Have I made them do that? Have I leaned over them too much? Especially if you've got little dogs, if you're leaning over all the time, they're kind of like, 'Whoa, big person leaning over. Not good.' It can be perceived as a little bit threatening, and quite often, you'll find that they shake off after.

If they're shaking off a lot, then start thinking about what's stressing them now.

I always tell them they're good, because it's so much better that they're calming themselves down, rather than us trying to teach them how do this. But just start to take a mental note of how often this is happening.

Let's have a look at a few basics of dog body language. The paw lift, the yawn, lip lick, look away, turn away, are all calming signals, as in they will use these signals to calm themselves, you or other dogs down. They will do all of these things, like very minor stress signals, but all things to look for. All things that you've probably not really noticed that much.

Yawning - of course dogs will yawn because they're tired, just like us, and they're the only other species that we can catch yawns from and that they can catch them from us, but they will yawn due to stress as well.

Stress signals - forward, upright stance, suspicious, maybe a bit anxious, scared, tucked under, quite small, low. Sweaty paws. Dogs do sweat through their pads, so if you've got, say, stone floors, then you'll be able to see when this starts to happen.

Stress release

Shake-off, the ground sniff and the scratch, usually of the collar when you walk in, and it's so annoying and you want to just carry on. They're all things that will help them calm down. You might find that they're ground sniffing because they want to sniff. It's all about context, but all things to start looking for.

Breed or breed type matters. Dogs are racist. Black dogs get a real bum deal. I love black dogs. I love nothing more than having a good cuddle with a big black dog, but because their whole face is in shadow, other dogs cannot read them as well. They can't tell what they're saying. So you'll probably find that if your dog's reacting badly to other dogs, they're going to be the worst with black dogs.

If your dog has folded ears, so what I mean is they're droopy ears. All of my guys have got droopy ears, but they can't communicate quite as well. If you think about the typical German Shepherd ears being very upright, you can see when they start to swivel, and if they're fully forward and very interested in something, or if they're pinned back and they're not very happy. Their ears do tell us a lot. If you've got a dog with folded ears, you will be able to see them twitching and moving and changing position, but obviously the other dogs can't read them as well as if they had upright ears.

Docked tails

A tail is a key way that dogs communicate with each other, so if they've been docked, for whatever reason ... No judgements here; if your dog's been docked and other dogs are reacting to your dog, a part of it could be that. If you've got, say, Bulldogs or dogs that are born without much of a tail, then that's restricting their ability to communicate. Short muzzles, so brachycephalic breeds such as Pugs, Bulldogs, Boxers, etc. they have very short muzzles. Their facial expressions are hard to see, they're on the back foot, so your dog might be worse with those kind of dogs, or if your dog is one of those dogs, other dogs can't read them as well.

Threatening or fearful possibly aggressive dog body language

Stiff slow movement, fast stiff short wags of the tail with it very high or very low.
Growls, snarls, front teeth showing.

Submissive, insecure, appeasing gestures (common in puppies under 16 weeks)

Rolling onto back showing belly, crawling on belly
Front paw lift
Lip licking the other dog

Low level stress signals

Yawning, panting, lip licking (own lips)

Mid/low level stress signals

Turning head away
Turning body away
Moving away

Rude behaviour when greeting (encourage away from another dog as they may get told off).

Going over the shoulder blades of the other dog
Jumping on the other dog's face or body
Barking in their face
Humping

16 CHILDREN AND DOGS

Teach new things that you will need first until you puppy is confident with it before letting the children do it

A common issue I see even when the kids and the dog are great together is that the kids have worn the pups name out! Pup soon learns to ignore its name, I'm sure you are the same with them at times... mum mum mum mum MUM! Or dad dad dad DAD! If this is happening be sure to revisit the name game and consider not letting children blow the whistle for recall so it doesn't get blown too much and pup learns to start ignoring it.

Kids can make brilliant trainers as they are very clear in their body language and dogs love to party at any moment.

It's very special growing up with a dog. The memories that are cherished and will shape your adult choices when it comes to dogs and animals - both positive and negative.

Gone are the days where it was common knowledge that you didn't approach the dog while it was eating or sleeping - now it seems dogs are labelled aggressive or bad if they show any reluctance to these advances and they must have a bad temperament if they growl when bounced on when sleeping or eating.

If we must live by this kind of mentality, then I should be locked up as I would definitely display and show my anger at being woken suddenly by someone prodding poking or jumping on me.

Teaching our children some key rules around dogs and some basic dog body language will help everyone and reduce negative interactions.

The rules to teach children

- Never touch a dog without asking the owner first
- Always keep away from busy dogs, bored dogs, dogs that are ill, or dogs that are tied up
- Never touch a loose dog
- Never make sudden movements when close to a dog
- Keep quiet and calm around dogs
- Never tease a dog. Never pull its ears, tail or fur. Dogs may not find it funny
- Only play with a dog when an adult is nearby
- Do not kiss or put your face near a dog - even your own dog. Never let a dog lick your face
- Never touch a dog that is sleeping
- Don't cuddle your dog too much - remember that dogs can feel smothered too
- Never eat when close to a dog
- Never go near a dog when it is on its own territory. If your ball accidentally goes over someone's fence, always ask an adult for help. Do not attempt to get the ball back yourself. Remember that dogs defend their own territory
- Never stare at a dog
- Never leave a young child alone with a dog
- Never touch a dog that is with its puppies
- Never run from a dog, screaming and waving your arms around
- Never ignore a dog's warning growl
- Always wash your hands after touching a dog
- If a dog jumps up at you or you are frightened by a dog then be a tree. Stand still and do not move

Routine is so important when you are raising a puppy alongside kids.

It's really common for pup to become crazed in the evenings and at weekends, but fine when the kids are at school, why is this?

When the house is busier, pup is on the go more and following and watching everyone, they sleep less and then become over tired and over stimulated. If this is happening it's really important to have structured downtime for pup to settle and relax and sleep and the kids to leave them alone. This maybe a chew or a Kong in their crate, pen or a quiet area. Short periods of rest and then re-joining the family will help reduce the boisterous antics.

What if pup is becoming a nuisance when the kids are on the trampoline or playing ball games in the garden?

Employ some management solutions when you can't be training them to do what you want instead. If this means shutting pup in the house for a while then that's ok, better that than them getting well practiced at becoming over excited at the kids jumping around and they can't control themselves and nip the ankle of your child's best friend from school, just because pup was too excited to know it wasn't playing.

Always consider what you would like them to do instead of run and chase. This maybe relaxing in a down position watching the kids from a distance or it may be that they are happy to play with their own toys when other things are happening. Set them up to succeed and practice this in short bursts with them, a nice comfy bed on the lawn and a chew to keep them occupied, practicing settle while you sit and read a book next to them and keeping an eye on the kids would be a great way to start this.

Toddlers and dogs

Raising toddlers and dogs together can be safe and wonderful for both, IF you are an alert and consistent parent! No matter how carefully you've taught the baby to 'pet the puppy nice' NEVER trust your young child alone with your dog or puppy, EVER. No matter how gentle or well-trained you think your child is, when you're not looking, the child is wanting to do all of the things you won't let him do when you're around!

PRO-ACTIVE SAFETY MEASURES –

Supervision, SUPER-vision, Super-VISION!

If you see the baby closing in on the unsuspecting dog, intercept him! Cornered dogs have no other choice but to tell the child to go away the only way they know how. Help them out of the situation before they have to. Surprise is one of the biggest reasons dogs spin and snap. A sudden reach, an impulsive hug, a handful of fur clenched tightly in a baby's fist or twisted lip or ear. Babies lose their balance and fall. You have to be there to catch them before they land on the sleeping dog!

Think of a dog as a pair of pointy scissors. If you leave the room, take the kid or the dog with you or put it in its crate, exercise pen, kitchen behind a baby gate or some other place where he can't leave and the kids can't go.

Teach the child to respect the dog's space. Interrupt and redirect if the dog uses the kids for a jungle gym or the kids treat the dog like a stuffed animal. No pony rides ever! Teach your children from day one that the dog is not a toy. Children should never approach a sleeping dog, an eating dog, a dog with a toy or chewie, a dog who is tired, a dog who isn't feeling well, a dog who is worried or excited, a dog who has had enough petting for one millennium. Watch the kids and the puppy to make sure neither are acting inappropriately and that they are respecting each other's space. If not, then they lose the privilege of being together. Time-outs are as effective with puppies as they are with children.

Be aware of how the DOG is feeling. You want your dog to adore the baby, respect the baby, maybe even protect the baby. But their relationship is a two-way street. Make sure that both are enjoying every interaction. If they aren't, it's your job to step in.

Safe Haven: If you have small children or someone else's kids come to visit, create a safe place for your dog. Use a baby gate or something that the dog can get over or through that the child cannot. When the dog does not want to be bothered by the child, show him he can escape to his safe place, and everything will be fine

Never put the dog in the position of needing to correct the kids. Your dog deserves respect and peace and quiet. Kids don't appreciate being pestered constantly by their siblings and neither does your dog. When, day after day, the polite signals are ignored, the puppy eventually gives them up as useless and just goes straight to what works - snarl-snap and, if necessary, bite. *77% of all bites to children are to the face* - probably because that's the part of the body that is invading and hugging and kissing and because a muzzle pin (open mouth across the offending pup's face) is how adult dogs correct invasive puppies. Your dog views small kids as pesky puppies.

Turn your back for even a moment, and your child will be a child - and your dog will be a dog! If the dog is not able to get away from the thing that annoys or terrifies him, remember that 'Plan B' is to try to get that thing away from HIM. The dog communicates that he wants to be left alone by looking away, moving away, showing his teeth and growling, all of which are proper social signals to avoid REAL aggression: biting. However, children are not dogs, and do not understand or heed this language, so it's important to BE THERE to intervene and give the dog a place to go where the child absolutely cannot follow. Again, this is where parenting and supervision are crucial to keep dog and child safe!

Individual breeds and individual dogs of the same breed have different temperaments and tolerance thresholds. Some are exceedingly patient and have a high pain tolerance and can put up with more abuse than others. Big, strong 'dive into ice cold water without noticing' and 'run through stickers and brambles without noticing' Labradors fall into this category ... but even these dogs have a limit and no dog should be forced to endure pain or torment in the name of being 'good with kids'. Well-socialised and trained dogs can be fine with gentle, respectful kids, but won't tolerate eternal pestering; hair pulling and 'over-loving' that is typical of young kids and toddlers.

Teach the dog to respect the child's space. Body awareness can be taught. 'Careful, easy, slow'. A child can have a great time enjoying the company of a considerate and respectful dog.

- **Set the speed limit** - the appropriate level of play. No jumping on the bed or banking off the couch. This is not road race 5000. All chase games, wresting games, and ball games are outside games.
- **Enforce stop signs and no trespassing signs.** There may be places in your house your dog is not allowed. He doesn't need free reign. This also extends to high chairs and peanut butter sandwiches clutched in tiny hands.
- **Provide a parking spot.** A crate, a bed, a time-out and settle-down zone. Failure to follow the rules or exceeding the speed limit gets him sent to the parking garage immediately; do not pass go, do not collect £200.
- **There may be special speed limits around school or hospital zones.** Don't underestimate your dog's ability to understand the concept of 'be careful around the baby' or 'don't trip grandma' or even 'watch your tail around the coffee table'.

Remember - just because your dog likes grown-ups, doesn't mean he automatically loves children. If his early puppyhood didn't include kind and gentle children, he may see them as scary little screaming aliens.

If you are concerned about your child's safety, get professional help immediately.

Pup is chasing and nipping the Children

Four things to do when your dog chases and nips at kids

Dogs and kids can be the best of playmates. Sometimes they develop this relationship all on their own, and sometimes they need some outside assistance to become fast friends. It's not uncommon for the basic dog-kid foundation to be solid, with just a few rough edges that need smoothing. One of the common rough spots is when your excited dog wants to chase after and nip your excited children. Here are five things you can do if your canine youngster wants to play a little too roughly with your human youngsters:

1.) Supervise: Dog trainers say it all the time: **Never leave small children alone with even the most trustworthy dog.** If you're present when play starts to escalate out of control, step in and calm things down. Without your intervention, your dog gets reinforced for her inappropriate behaviour. Chasing a squealing child is a very fun game! – at least for the dog, and sometimes for the child – until a bite happens. Behaviours that are reinforced are more likely to be repeated and to increase in intensity, and are harder to modify or extinguish. Even the most kid-loving dog can get too excited... Protect your dog and your kids by banning chasing games.

2.) Make rules: Of course children need to be able to run around without worrying about a canine ambush. Set some firm house rules that are designed to minimise chase-and-nip games. If your dog loves kids, its fine to allow your small children and their friends to hang out with the dog (under direct supervision, of course), your older children and their friends can hang out with the dog with less supervision. In either case, one house rule should be that before rowdy play happens, the dog gets escorted to a safe place away from the action, and gets something wonderful (i.e. stuffed Kong) so she doesn't feel punished. Another house rule is 'absolutely no deliberately antagonising the dog to encourage her to chase or nip'. Violation of these rules should result in loss of dog-companionship privileges for a pre-determined period.

3.) Train your dog: The better-trained your dog is, the easier it is for you to calmly and quickly intervene. A gentle 'come' or 'down' cue for a dog that is under good stimulus control is all it takes to abort the chase-and-nip game. Deliver high-value rewards when your wonderful dog responds immediately to your cue to keep those responses strong. Behaviours that are reinforced are more likely to repeated and repeated with enthusiasm.

4.) Teach your children well: The best way to train your children to interact appropriately with your dog is to include them in your dog's training program. You can teach even very young children how to elicit a polite sit from your dog by raising their hands to their chest – if you've taught your dog this body-language signal to sit. Teach your young humans how to play 'trade' with your dog by offering a treat or a toy to get her to give up something she has in her mouth, then encourage them to play games that direct her energy – and her teeth – toward something other than a child's skin or clothing, such as a ball or Frisbee. The better you are at teaching your children what to do (and reinforcing them for it!), the more they will do what you want them to. Just like dogs!

17 HOW DO THEY LEARN BEST?

Quick tips to get the best results when training

3 minutes! Concentration, environments and distractions

When is it best to start training with my puppy?

Training is the process of teaching and the student learning. In the case of puppies, they are the eternal student, and the trainer/teacher is the world around them, not just you.

An 8 week old puppy is a little sponge constantly absorbing information, sometimes not the information you want them to learn either!

The short answer is start teaching them and training them what you do want from the moment they come home, housetraining, where they are allowed and not allowed to go and also how to sit, what their name is etc.

I have trained numerous 5 week old puppies, still with their littermates and mum how to sit, wait, respond to their name and to look at me.

No, your puppy is not too young to start training!

Training does not mean they cannot have fun and enjoy puppyhood. You are not being the fun police; training means you start bonding quicker and makes your life easier together right from the start. If anything, training from a young age allows them more freedom and fun.

The trick (no pun intended) is to keep things brief and keep it fun!

Just 3 minutes each time! For puppies or adult dogs, it's been proven that little spurts of training and often is better than longer periods. Puppies can't concentrate for long and I'm sure you will be tired from all the other bits of caring for pup too.

When you boil the kettle to make a hot drink just train puppy until it boils, or when the adverts come on if you are watching TV.

If like me you are finding yourself getting carried away and training for longer than say 5 minutes each time, then use a timer on your phone or use an egg timer to keep you on track!

Puppy may still be keen to carry on after 3 minutes but it's always best to leave them wanting more rather than training until they switch off or get bored. Alternatively, just put 15 little, tiny morsels of treats to one side and work through them in training one by one then do something else, finishing the session.

What's even better is training will really tire your puppy out, 10 minutes training is equivalent to an hour walk! You can't walk puppy that far while they are young and certainly you should not be walking them for an hour, so this is a great way to ensure you get some peace too.

So now you have been practicing sit, down and look at you etc. for a while and you are now trying to get them to do it when you take them to your friend's house and you are trying to show off a little, but puppy looks at you blankly as if you have never taught them these things before, you get frustrated and disheartened.

Why does this happen?

This is totally normal, because dogs don't generalise well. What this means is once you have taught something new at home, inside and out in the garden then try and do it somewhere else they think well I'm not where I normally am, so I don't understand what you are asking me to do.

How do we help them?

Whenever we are asking something of them that they have learnt before but in a new environment or place, we take it back a few steps to remind them and then we can progress quicker through the training steps than what we did originally teaching the exercise. They need to find confidence, so making things easier will help them and remind them that even though things are different we still would like them to do the same thing.

You need to practice everything in at least 5 different situations/places/environments before you can start to expect them to know what you mean and want from them wherever you take them.

The other thing to consider is how distracted they are. Going from doing a sit stay at home when it's quiet and the kids are in bed is very different to being on a busy high street with people and dogs walking by all the time.

This is often why you may find the first week or two at training classes difficult as your puppy is so excited and distracted by everything going on around them at class.

We should always try and built up distractions slowly, starting with distractions far away and then when we have success, we gradually ask them to do it again with the distractions closer and closer. Baby steps and lots of practice really works!

If you find that they are struggling to focus, then just get more distance away from the distractions (most often people and other dogs), ensure they have a few repetitions where they have got it right before then slowly trying to make it a little harder for them again. The closer they are to something they want, the more likely they are to ignore you and want to go investigate the distraction.

Remember to always try and set them up for success, make things really easy for them to win and hard for them to get wrong. This was of training makes for a confident, willing and eager to please pooch.

Keep it brief, set them up to win and keep it fun for both of you!

Treats and rewards/wages

Ok so I'll hold my hands up and admit I am primarily a food reward and hand signals/body language trainer with my own dogs.

What do I mean by that?

I use food as my dog's wages to train them more than I use toys or physical praise as their reward for doing what I want.

Why?

Because it's the quickest easiest way to get the results you want and if truth be known I am all for the quickest simplest way to get what I want.

I am lazy so if there is a quicker easier way to do things with dogs I promise you, I have found it and will share it with you.

Would you get out of bed to go to work without being paid? Likely not!

Even I wouldn't and I adore my job but let's face it we all want to have a life and relax but performing a task for rewards allows us to do this, employing this mentality when it comes to our pups, at least while they are still growing, and maturing is a great way to ensure an easier life.

Hand signals and body language

In fear of saying the obvious, dogs don't speak English, do they? And yes of course they do learn what certain words mean such as sit, stay etc. Through training they will learn through gestures, hand signals and our body language and expression first and they are so in tune with this because this is easier for them to learn than those strange sounds that come from our lips.

If you truly want to understand the magic of rewards and using them to the best advantage then read on.

Considering the value of the reward, what type and how we use them

Whenever we are teaching anything new to our dogs, we should be using rewards. Some behaviours we ask of them need rewarding regularly throughout their lives too, not just while we are teaching it.

Rewards can come in many forms – treats, toys, physically stroking the dog and verbal praise are usually the main ones. Think about environmental rewards too, if your dog likes a good tear around off lead and it's safe to do so you can use that as a reward, just like if your dog enjoys a good sniff of a particular spot you can use that too. Think outside the box!

How do we tell what value the reward has to our dog? And does this matter?

As I do in many areas of my training, I like to look at things from a human perspective. Would we go to work, for an eight hour shift for just 50p? No! However, we do get up and go to work for a decent wage, a wage that is worthwhile to us and our lifestyles. Without the right wage packet, we would start looking elsewhere for other jobs that would give us this.

Back to looking at our dogs, if we aren't giving the right value of reward (or wages) our dogs find something else to do that is rewarding enough - often going and playing with another dog, chasing a squirrel or finding some lovely au de fox poo to anoint himself with after you have asked him not to.

I will always prefer cake over chocolate, that's not to say I don't like chocolate, because I do, but I would much rather have a tiny slice of cake over a whole slab of chocolate any day. This is because I value cake over chocolate. Every dog is different with this. – I have worked with one dog who valued a piece of strawberry over anything else, even cooked liver. Most dogs will value liver, fish or heart over most other treats, but this is not all dogs.

With my own dogs I always have at least three different types of food rewards when training, they all value food over most other types of reward, but if I always gave them their favourite reward every time it wouldn't be as rewarding anymore (just like if I binged on cake every day I would get to the point where I was bored with the taste and start looking to other foods to enjoy). Having three different rewards to hand makes it a guessing game to my dogs when their favourite will be dispensed and keeps them working harder for longer in expectation of 'it might be this time I get it'.

If you are just using low value treats such as dry, not so smelly treats and they do something well or work extra hard, then don't be tight, give them a handful! (i.e. for us a hand full of 50p coins would add up).

What food types and toys does your dog get more excited over? What do they like, what do they go crazy for?

A good way to try with toys is to get all of your dog's toys out and see which they go to first and prefer over the others. Then remove that toy, what do they go for next? You can also do this in your local pet shop by putting some toys on the floor to see which they go to first and keep trying to go back for.

How can you increase or decrease the value of the same reward?

Let's take a dry treat or a piece of kibble as an example, for most dogs this is a reward but pretty low value (much like a 50p to us, we aren't going to say no but if given the option of 50p or a £20 note we wouldn't choose the 50p).

Feeding it from your hand = 50p. Throwing it in the air, hiding it or rolling it on the floor for a dog to catch or chase or hunt for = anything up to £10. Breeds such as Spaniels, hounds and hunting types will find the hunting for it very rewarding as they are using their natural instincts at the same time.

How you use a toy can increase or decrease the value of it too. Waving a toy in a dog's face for many dogs can be very off putting, but if thrown or offered in expectation of a good old game of tug of war can really ignite a dog's playful streak. Hiding a toy, either in long grass, under a rock or behind the sofa will change the value of the reward also.

I'm sure you have all experienced one of your own dogs losing a toy under the sofa and them going crazy to get it but once you have helped them to get it, they lose interest pretty quickly. That frustration of it just being out of reach increases the desire to have the item, without further interaction with the toy, it's pretty boring for most dogs. While I'm not suggesting you encourage your dogs to ruin your sofa by scratching to get under it, this hopefully highlights that finding hide and seek with toys is a very easy and fun thing to do with your dog.

You can also decrease the value of a toy or a treat by using the same thing in the same way all of the time. If you always use the same type of food to reward your dog, for example always using the same brand and type of cheese and in the same sized chunks, over time your dog will start to value it less because it gets it so often.

The same applies to toys, if you are using for example the same ball for every play session as a reward and the dog has access to that ball all of the time it will be less interested in playing with it as time progresses as it isn't that exciting anymore.

Having a toy that your dog loves, and you only get it out for play time and then put it out of the way after will help hold the value of that toy for longer. If however, you did this same thing with a selection for 3-4 toys (putting them away after) you will have more ways to reward your dog and they will keep their value for longer. Your dog having access to toys around the house is a good thing, but these are not necessarily the toys to use when training as a reward.

Fading those rewards, how do we start to step away from treats and play once the dog knows what we are asking?

Are you ready for this stage yet? Can your dog perform the task you have trained in every environment or place you expect it to? Can your dog do it if you are not waving the treat or toy in its face first? Could you bet £50 on the dog doing it the first time you ask, every time? If the answer is no to any of the above, you need to go back and work on those before progressing to this step.

How do we transition from feeding or playing with our dog every time they do this new thing we have trained and asked them to do, to not? There are many ways to do this but the main three are as follows –

Random Rewards: when I say random, I mean just that!

Stage 1 - randomly not rewarding your dog, but you are rewarding them more often than not.

Stage 2 - this is rewarding your dog the first time, the second, then the fifth, tenth time etc. This builds the anticipation to the dog that when they perform what you have asked, it might just be this time they get the reward. When starting stage 2 my best advice is to use higher value treats or if using a toy for play use their absolute favourite or make the toy you have been using more valuable by hiding it (if this is what your dog likes) or by playing for longer.

Lessen the Value: in other words, we are paying less wages now they know what we expect. Rewarding every time, as before but if you are using treats then use a lower value or less smelly or smaller piece/quantity. Use a less interesting toy or play for less time.

Jackpot Rewards: occasionally give your dog a handful of treats, a whole chicken breast! Have a big game with your dog, be silly, dance around with them with their favourite toy in the whole world, get them excited and silly too. This is something I do with my dogs around every 4-6 months for coming back when called on a walk, when there are no distractions, so it couldn't get much easier for them, even with my adult dogs. Imagine that feeling you would have if you won the lottery, you play and pay your money every week, sometimes win a tenner if you are lucky and then every six months or so you happen to win the jackpot! You would certainly keep going and buying a ticket every week, wouldn't you?

The three methods above are not mutually exclusive, and you will see the best results by swapping and changing all of them, regularly.

Don't rush this part in your training. If someone was to half your wages overnight, you are pretty much guaranteed to not work as hard, you might turn up and appear to work but your heart wouldn't be in it, and not much would get done. If, however you were given a little wage cut (lessen the value) but promised a big bonus (jackpot reward) if you worked hard, you would be more likely to continue to work as before, if not work a little harder on the off chance you might get that bonus today.

Take it slow and enjoy the bonding process throughout.

Timing of rewards, using rewards when we don't mean to and selective reward to improve what we want even more

Timing is everything!

A common thing I see with puppies and puppy owners in particular is when training sit, and they end up with this frustrating jumping up behaviour. It goes a little like this – owner asks for sit, dog sits, owner gets treat and starts to place their hand toward the dog to give them the treat, the dog jumps up to meet the treat halfway and gets the treat. Problem? The dog is getting rewarded for the jumping up and starts to associate the word sit with jumping up. Dogs will only perceive the reward is for that they are doing at that split second, sometimes the split second before but it's handy to remember that dogs do what works if they are getting rewarded then whatever they are doing at that moment is more likely to be repeated again. If you think you have been rewarding at the wrong time, then simply take a step back, make it even easier for the dog to get it right and start rewarding for what you do want. Clicker training is an excellent way to sharpen up your timing and also gives you more time to reward your dog.

When your dog plays the clown

If you find yourself laughing at your dog, for maybe doing something a little naughty but in a cheeky way – this is a reward for your dog. Now I have yet to try training a dog and its only reward is my laughter and I'm sure this would not work, but our laughter certainly encourages behaviours to be repeated. Is what you are laughing at something you want more of? If so, then yes chuckle and reward with treats and play to encourage repetition. If not distract your dog and do something else which should also focus you (and help stop the laughter). I would also consider if this comical behaviour was amplified, whether in duration, volume (of applicable) or frequency - would this cause a problem?

Selective rewards

I talked about 'jackpot rewards' – giving a handful of treats or having a longer play session. We can also apply jackpot rewards to improving anything we are training even further, if your dog has done something very well, has worked particularly hard or had a lightbulb moment by maybe putting two things together (this does happen!) then give them the world, make them feel like they have won the lottery. You can also lessen the rewards for average effort on the part of the dog and pay him well for trying that bit harder!

In summary, rewards can be magical, as can your training! Have fun with your dog and pay him well. You don't have to be a professional dog trainer to get amazing results and an amazing bond with your dog.

18 HOW TO TEACH THEM

House/toilet training

Toilet training and general tips and tricks in the early phases

Puppies only have a very tiny, weak bladder, which means that they have to go to the loo a lot! Basically, your puppy will need to go to the loo as soon as he wakes up in the morning, whenever he wakes up from a sleep, after he has eaten food, whenever he has had a play session, last thing at night and about every 30 minutes or so during the day.

Watch, watch, watch!

The key to successful house training is supervision. Watch your dog constantly. Your first duty is to identify what your dog does right before it eliminates. Does your dog sniff? Circle? Hold his ears in a certain position? Some dogs provide signals that are easy to spot, while others are more difficult. Watch carefully. If you are using paper, when he pees on the paper and you put clean paper down, put a little bit of the wet paper on the clean paper, then it will encourage him to go back to the paper because he can smell his scent there.

Praise, praise, praise!

When you see the signs of an impending puddle, react! Quickly -

before he has the chance to squat - ask him in an excited voice, 'Do you want to go OUT?' Lead the way, continuing to praise all the way. Once outside, stay with him until you witness the desired results and praise him straight after he has performed 'Good, go wee/poo!' Make him feel that he is the most special dog in the whole world.

Confine when you can't watch. By confining him to a small place, like a crate or pen, you will teach him to wait to be let out. He will be more reluctant to soil his crate, because if he does, he will be forced to sit and look at it and smell it until you return. When you do let him out, take him directly to his assigned toilet area and praise for quick results.

Keep a regular schedule. Take him out first thing in the morning, last thing at night, every time he has eaten, every time he has had a play session and many times in between. Feed and exercise on a regular schedule. Remember, what goes in regularly, will come out regularly. How soon after he eats does he need to go out? Keep track. Free choice feeding may hamper your house training efforts - what trickles in will trickle out unpredictably! Your dog will probably need to go out soon after eating, after napping, and after exercising. If you can anticipate when he needs to go and hustle him to the appropriate spot at the first sign, you'll avoid accidents.

Don't just put him out, stay with him. If you don't stay, you'll miss the chance to praise and you'll also miss the chance to name the behaviour. 'Outside' is where he needs to go, 'Toilet', 'Find a tree', or 'Do your business' (call it what you like) is what he needs to do when he gets there. If you stay with him, you'll also know for a fact that both duties were accomplished before he comes back in. (You'll also be glad that your dog is comfortable eliminating in your presence when you're standing in the rain at the motorway services on the way to your holiday with your pet!)

He comes right back in and makes a mess. If you leave him out alone, you won't know if he completed his assigned tasks or was distracted by a butterfly. Many young puppies are distraught about being separated from their owners. They may spend the entire time while outside just sitting on the porch. It's unlikely that your pup will want to ask to go outside if it is a negative experience to be separated from the security of its human family. 'He was out for two hours and came in immediately made a mess.' He may have spent most of the past two hours napping, awoke to the sound of the door and came running. Now he's finally back inside - is he going to want to ask to be left out again?

No Punishment. If he has an accident, swat yourself with the rolled up newspaper, not the dog. It was your fault for not watching him closely enough! Rubbing his nose in it (an age old myth), scolding or hitting will only teach him to avoid you when he feels the need, rather than come find you. Correcting before the dog learns how to ask only teaches the dog to sneak off down the hall or behind the sofa where you won't see him.

Teach him how to ask. If you have been a good cheerleader, your dog has probably made the association between the feeling of a full bladder and your excitement at the prospect of going outside. You may notice that he circles and then looks to you like, 'Well? I'm feeling it - are you going to get excited?' Now is the time to start playing 'silly'. 'What? What do you want? Show me!' The sillier you appear, the more explicit he will be when trying to communicate his needs. Before you know it, he will be asking.

Accidents happen. Upsets in schedule, changes in food, or illness may contribute to temporary lapses in housetraining. See your veterinarian if it persists. Outside stresses, changes in weather, a new pet or baby in the family, may also upset your dog's toilet habits. Punishing long after the fact will only add to his stress. Back up, give him more structure, confine and supervise. Help him be good!

Further toilet training tips

Puppy does not have control over their bladder till they are 12 weeks of age. Before this age it is certainly worth putting the time and energy in to shape and make good habits and start as you mean to go on. If there is the odd accident, even if you have been consistent watching like a hawk and taking them out every 20-30 minutes don't worry too much, accidents happen!

Cleaning products – always use an enzyme-based cleaner for pets! Using Dettol or anti-bac or disinfectant isn't enough. Of course, you can use any of these products as well as an enzyme cleaner, but these products alone will not remove the scent for the puppy, and they are likely to return to the same spot again.

Puppy pads/newspaper etc... to use or not?

As much as possible right from the day puppy comes home, taking them out in the garden to toilet is best, rather than them learn its ok to go in the house (even if it is on a puppy pad). However, if you have a pen and crate set up then having a puppy pad in the pen area for extended periods that you are unable to be there (overnight or if you have to go out for a couple of houses) is a good idea. Though I tend to take these away when puppy gets to 12-14 weeks provided the routine is there, you have had no accidents for a week and puppy is going through the night without using the pads or paper.

Puppy is chewing the puppy pads? There are puppy pad holders available to purchase which will help prevent this, they will frame the pad with a plastic edge.

Puppy is going successfully outside when I take them but then come inside and continue to do their business straight away?

You may have been a little too eager to praise them for performing and interrupted them, mid flow. Puppies are so easily distracted! Try and wait till you are confident they have finished performing before telling them how good they are and rewarding them.

How should you react if you find puppy 'going' while in the house?

If you see them having an accident (the key thing here is that you are actually witnessing it happen). Don't say a word, calmly and quietly pick them up and take them outside, wait out there with them for them to perform again. Reward as you normally would when they do perform outside.

It will be really tempting to shout or get annoyed when this happens, especially if you have been making great progress and you feel like this is a setback. Take a deep breath and follow my instructions above. If you shock, scold or scare them at this point they will learn very quickly to find somewhere out of sight and hide to toilet, this could be behind a sofa, under furniture and other places where you may not notice straight away or know how long this has been going on for.

Remember if you can't watch them, it's best to confine them in a small area so they are less likely to toilet. Housetraining is hard work and constant for a few weeks. You will get there!

Large breed male puppies I find are the easiest and quickest to house train and it's a sliding scale down to small breed females being the hardest to housetrain – but certainly not impossible!

Another thing I have found, for which I have no scientific evidence of just my own findings and with client's dogs – male puppies, if you remove puppy from sight when you clear up the accident this seems to help speed up the housetraining, rather than letting them watch you clear up their little puddle.

Crate training

Step by step

Puppy crate training is a fantastic method of managing the safety and well-being of young puppies. When used properly the crate is an invaluable tool for establishing good habits in your puppies and also for preventing problem behaviours before they arise.

Why do we do it?

Over time the crate will become your puppy's own private area which they will grow to love and feel secure in. You will come to rely on your crate just like I do in many day to day activities including:

- One of the first and most important uses of the crate is in the puppy housebreaking process. Crate training is the best way to quickly teach your puppy to eliminate (go to the toilet) outside.
- Crating our puppies teaches them to chew on the toys we provide to them and prevents them from chewing on the things we don't want them to chew on (shoes, furniture, curtains etc.). This is the key to establishing good habits in our dogs and preventing destructive habits which can be difficult to rectify.
- When your young puppy is in his crate he is safe from any number of dangerous household items. Unfortunately, many puppies are severely injured and killed every year as a result of chewing wires, ingesting poisons or eating foreign objects.
- Separation anxiety is a huge problem for an increasingly large percentage of dogs. Proper use of the crate can help reduce the chance of your puppy developing separation anxiety. The crate becomes a place where your dog is calm, out of trouble and accustomed to being alone. I should add here that if you are away from home all day every day is a puppy really suitable for someone with your lifestyle anyway?

Never Ever Use Your Crate as A Tool for Punishment!

- If you have friends or visitors of any kind coming and going from your home the crate is the perfect place to keep your puppy safely confined for a while.
- Because most crates are lightweight and portable you can move them from room to room so your puppy can be close by you all day long!
- Many crates are suitable for putting into your car which

makes your puppy's traveling experience safer and often less stressful.

- When your puppy grows to love his crate, it makes trips and stays at places such as your vet and dog groomers a more bearable experience.
- When puppy crate training is applied correctly your puppy cannot get into any mischief which significantly reduces any need to discipline him. This makes for a far better environment in which to live (for both dog and owner).
- If you plan to do any activities like competitive obedience training, fly-ball or agility training you will find your crate is a great place to confine your dog in between training sessions and competition. Put it in a nice cool spot in the shade.

Selecting a crate for your puppy

The crates basically come in three general styles; durable plastic, fabric mesh and an all wire mesh type, which is often collapsible. It's really a personal choice which style of crate you go for, but the most important thing is that you buy one that is the appropriate size for your dog. Get a crate that will be large enough for your fully grown puppy and partition it off until he grows into it. Most good pet shops sell good quality crates and there are many good online sites; just Google dog crates. Be aware that puppies can chew and claw their way out of a fabric style crate so I would always start with a metal or plastic one till they are relaxed and happy to settle in a crate.

Apart from the dog what else goes in the crate?

1. Bedding - choose a nice comfortable dog bed that can't be chewed up and swallowed by your feisty little pup. Be sure to choose bedding suited to your climate.
2. Chew toys - get a couple of good chew toys that you can stuff and even freeze. This keeps your puppy busy and teaches him what is appropriate to chew on. My dogs love Kongs and Buster Cubes.
3. Water - keep a nice supply of clean fresh water. Heavy wide

based bowls that won't be tipped over are best or you can buy one that clips securely onto the crate wall.

Where is best to put the crate?

Ideally away from large windows and doorways, so puppy feels safe.

I like to use a crate with a puppy pen around it, but you may opt to just use a crate which is fine too.

Introducing your puppy to the crate

Your puppy's first impression and experiences with the crate are all important. We need to set it up so your puppy views the crate as a positive object right from the start. You goal is for your puppy to love the crate and choose to use it himself rather than as a contraption he associates with isolation and loneliness. Try some of the puppy crate training tips below to make the crate inviting to your puppy - always take it slowly. Put the crate in the room with you and your puppy and leave the crate door open, wide.

1. Drop a few tasty treats in and around the crate and let your puppy clean them up. Be sure to give heaps of encouragement and then praise if your puppy bravely steps into the crate.
2. If your puppy has a favourite dog bed or blanket put this inside the crate to encourage him and to make it more homely for him.
3. Feed your puppy all of his meals in the crate (door still open).
4. With your puppy outside the crate place a chew toy inside the crate and close the door. Your puppy will literally beg you to let him at it! Open up the door, let him in and praise his efforts (this method has proved very successful for my dogs).
5. When your puppy is not around, put a chew toy (like a stuffed Kong) inside the crate and leave the door open. Let

him discover the 'treasure' and leave him inside to enjoy the find.

6. When your puppy is comfortable in the crate close the door and feed some treats to him through the mesh. To start with just leave the door closed for 10 seconds then gradually increase the duration. Don't increase the time too quickly, if your dog becomes distressed or whines you are moving too fast.

7. Build up the amount of time he is in the crate slowly, first when you are in the room, then step outside the room for a short time. Your puppy's first really long stretch in the crate is ideally overnight with the crate in your bedroom.

Shaping the behaviour

I find that the tips outlined above are more than enough to get most puppies comfortable in their crates. If you are having trouble with a difficult or nervous pup, try this puppy crate training exercise to shape the desired behaviour.

1. Place the crate in an area where you and your puppy spend time together - leave the crate door open.

2. Any time your puppy shows any interest in the crate (like a look) praise him and throw him a tasty treat. Repeat this over and over.

3. You'll find that your puppy soon becomes very interested in his crate. This step asks more of your puppy. Don't praise and treat only a glance at the crate now, wait until your pup walks over towards the crate, then enthusiastically praise and reward with a treat.

4. Repeat Step 3 many times and then make it harder again for your puppy to earn a treat. Hold off with your praise and treats until your puppy actually steps in the crate now. Repetition and reinforcing the desired behaviour is the key.

5. Now your pup should be popping in and out of the crate to work for his treats. Now you hold off with your praise and treats until your puppy goes into the crate and sits down.

6. The final step is to have your puppy step inside the crate, sit down and then you will close the crate door (only for a few

seconds to start with) and feed some treats through the door.

7. Attach a cue word to this process such as 'bedtime' or 'go to crate'. Say your cue word every time your puppy steps inside the crate - he will soon associate the word with the act of getting into the crate.

General rules of puppy crate training

- Always take your dog's collar off when he is put in the crate. Otherwise, the collar can get caught on the crate which can have disastrous consequences.

- Ensure that you aren't asking your puppy (or older dog for that matter) to hold off from going to the toilet for longer than she is physically capable.

- If your puppy does have a toilet accident inside his crate obviously punishment is not an option, but you should be angry at yourself. Immediately clean up the mess including the use of an odour neutraliser.

- Be careful when crating your puppy in hot weather. Be especially careful when you have your puppy crated in your car, temperatures can become extreme inside cars and in a very short period of time.

- Except for overnight and one off occasions you should never crate your dog for more than 4 or 5 hours at a time. Why have a dog if you have to confine him for such long periods? Perhaps a goldfish would be more suitable? If you work an 8 hour day, try coming home at lunch to let your dog out for a little bit, or pay a professional dog walker to walk your dog during the day, to at least break up the day for them.

- Dogs love their exercise, particularly nice long walks with you. So, if you are going to crate your puppy or older dog, they will require plenty of exercise and mental stimulation throughout the day. This can also include some little training sessions too.

- Never release your puppy from his crate (unless the situation is getting dangerous) if he is causing a fuss by whining, barking or being destructive. If you give in to these demands you are actually rewarding and therefore reinforcing this undesirable behaviour.

- Don't fall into the trap of only crating your puppy when you are about to leave the house - the crate will begin to be associated with you leaving if this is the case.

Good luck with your puppy crate training - as long as you follow the above plan with consistency and patience, I'm sure you'll achieve great results.

Crate games

Caveat –

These games are for once your dog is happy to be in a crate and isn't panicking at the door being shut.

All the following training exercises should be kept very short at first and always ensure your dog has been to the toilet shortly beforehand to ensure if they are trying to get out that it's not because they are uncomfortable and crossing their legs to go to the toilet.

Manners getting out / say please

Some manners and self-control getting out are essential once they are happy in their crate.

This is a very simple thing to train and can often be complete from start to finish in just one day by doing 3-4 short sessions.

When your dog is in the crate with the door shut and they are happy to be in their crate for periods of time.

This is key - this is something to teach AFTER you have done 'crate training'.

Ask your dog to sit or lay down as you approach the crate if they have stood up in anticipation of being released.

Reward them through the bars for the crate for doing as you have asked.

If they then stand up or move again then repeat and ask for a wait or stay. You can give them a few titbits at regular intervals for staying put, but only to 20-30 seconds.

As you move your hand toward the latch of the crate door you may need to repeat the command and reward if they do not move.

Repeat this until you can fiddle with the latch, it can make noise and your dog is waiting patiently and quietly.

The next step is to open the door slightly, only an inch or two and reward your dog for staying where they are despite the possibility of being able to push the door to freedom.

Practice this lots, and as your dog gets the idea that they stay where they are and get fed quite literally for doing nothing (well not nothing, they are using self-control, but you get my drift).

Gradually work to being able to have the door fully open with your dog staying in the crate and being still (wagging tail more than acceptable!).

Tips: keep closing the door and locking it between each repetition as this forms the full picture in the dog's mind

Move away from the crate once you have locked it and re approach regularly while practicing - again so your dog is getting used to the whole end picture.

At this stage do not ask your dog to come out of the crate, we are simply concentrating on working the door being open after a short period of them being confined in their cave and them staying within in it even when there is an opportunity to come out.

Troubleshooting

What if we go a little too fast too soon and the dog charges through the gap or goes to surge forward in an attempt to escape?

Don't worry. This will often happen while training. It's not what we want but we shouldn't give up at this point - simply ask your dog to return to the crate and go back a step or two, make it really easy for the dog to get it right, set him up to win and reward. Slow down how quickly you are going through the steps again.

If the dog goes to move forward without being asked you can also carefully use the crate door and shut it again - BEING CAREFUL NOT TO TRAP YOUR DOG IN THE GAP!

This should only be used occasionally if things are not going to plan... if you are finding yourself using this method more than a couple of times in the first two sessions of practicing this then you are going too fast in the training for your dog, slow it down again.

Once you have success of your dog being able to restrain itself when the door is wide open for a few seconds, a few times you can start to sometimes ask your dog to come out of the crate. If your dog is full of beans and is coming out of the crate at speed still, then a couple of treats placed on the floor just outside of the crate will start to slow him down and keep him near the crate and near you. Once his head comes back up after snaffling the treats on the floor ask him to sit or down outside of the crate and by you.

*If you have more than one dog, it would be useful at this point to ask your dog to sit and wait outside of the crate while you shut and lock the crate door to prevent the other dogs going in and investigating this fun cave that smells of treats.

Once you have success a few times of asking your dog to come out after self-control and then achieving control outside of the crate only practice the release one in three times, the other two times as before where the crate door is shutting.

Don't forget that once you have trained this that you should expect control each and every time you open the crate door.

Netflix and ~~chill~~ Crate

Your dog may not be used to relaxing in a crate while you are around and at home in the daytime.

Many dogs that have been crate trained will only be shut in there at night when you are going to bed or when you are leaving your dog at home and you leave for work etc.

Your dog learning to relax while you are at home, doing housework, relaxing in front of the TV and just generally mooching around at home is a very different thing.

If your dog is struggling then as well as chews, interactive toys, stuffed Kongs, lickimats etc. we can practice 'Netflix and Crate'.

Move the crate so it's next to the sofa or chair that you relax in when watching TV or read a book or flick through social media on your phone/tablet/laptop etc.

*You could also place the crate next to your desk if you are working and practice the same thing.

Think about how your dog normally sleeps or relaxes and in what position.

What is normal for him? What does the relaxed picture look like for your dog?

Do they rest their chin on their paws, hips rocked over to one side? Do they tuck one paw under their chest? Lay flat on their side? Legs akimbo upside down? Only you will know what is normal for your dog.

Have some small, low value treats to hand. Do not have these treats in a plastic bag or something that will make a noise every time you touch them.
 Dog and crate on one side of chair/sofa/desk etc. and treats on the other (ideally out of sight of the dog).

As you sit and watch TV or be preoccupied in some way or another, keep a watchful eye on your dog in your peripheral vision.

Initially - quietly and sneakily drop a treat through the top of the crate every time your dog takes a step toward being relaxed and not looking at you. Ideally you should be dropping the treat through the crate, so it falls just by their mouth, so they only have to make minimal movement to eat the treat.

It's important that we stay quiet (no talking to the dog) and reward the dog for NOT looking at you. This may feel quite backwards as most training we do involves the dog concentrating on us.

We want to start making incremental steps toward your dog truly relaxing and sleeping in their crate while you are 'busy' but present and in the same room. We do this by paying them at regular intervals and every time they are making steps toward that.

Your dog focusing on your every move isn't a dog in a relaxed and sleepy frame of mind. We want them to switch off so the timing of the award, the value of the reward to our dog and us being quiet are all key to success to this.

Consider the value of the treats you are using.

For this exercise low value treats are needed. Too high value, or too exciting means your dog will be anticipating the next treat too much and not relax.

All dogs will value different treats differently.

Just like I prefer cake over chocolate, I also like oaty biscuits, but I would rather have cake above all.

If I were to put myself in the dog's position here biscuits would be the best thing to train… if one landed in front of me, I would be 'oh thanks, nom'.

Chocolate 'ooh THANKS!'.

Cake 'OMG best day ever, CAKE! Amazing thank you!!! NOM! Anymore??'

For some dogs a low value treats maybe some of their normal kibble if they are fed on dry food, or a raw piece of carrot.

Feed often for the dog choosing to get comfy, stay comfy and then get comfier. All while you are appearing to be preoccupied.

Troubleshooting: if your dog is getting either excitable or making noise as they want to come out (assuming it's not for a toilet trip). Don't talk to them or make eye contact. Stay calm, don't get frustrated at them. Have patience and wait until they do something, anything that suggests they are starting to relax or switch off then reward.

Keep these sessions short initially; 5-10 minutes and then build up the time by practicing regularly.

Attention to name and focus on you

If you live in a home where there are kids running around, televisions blaring and everything happening all the time, lock yourself in the bathroom with your dog. Bring along some well-hidden treats. Have a seat. Do nothing. Wait for your dog to look at you. When he does give him a treat. Do this each time he looks at you, without calling or otherwise luring him. He should soon catch on and begin glancing at you more frequently. Once he's 'got it,' move to another low-distraction room in your house and start the exercise again. If you don't have distractions in the house to begin with, the kitchen is a wonderful room in which to start attention training. Ever notice how our companions seem to find us endlessly fascinating when we're in the vicinity of food?

After a few sessions, make the game a little harder. Hold a treat in your hand. As your dog watches, slowly extend the arm with the treat straight out to the side. Don't say a word. Your dog will likely track the movement of the treat, and then stare at it. Don't say a word and don't move. (That's the hard part!) He will eventually look at your face instead. The instant he does, tell him he's a good boy and treat. Vary holding the treat straight out, above your head, or anywhere else you can think of. (Just don't hold it too close to your dog.) Once he is reliably looking at you each time you hold the treat out, add his name *just as he begins to look at you*. When he does, treat! Once he's caught on, begin to say your dog's name just after holding out the treat but *before* he looks at you. Once he's got it, repeat this game in different locations.

'Huh? You are talking to me?'

You might assume that your dog knows his name. Great. But does he respond *each and every time you say it*? With these simple exercises, you are conditioning the reflex to look at you automatically and reliably each time you say his name. Do five to ten rapid repetitions, then break for 30 seconds or so. Repeat. Keep training sessions for attention no longer than 3 to 5 minutes. Pups will have a shorter attention span than adults, so keep puppy sessions to 2 to 3 minutes. Practice these exercises throughout the day, progressing slowly to areas with more distractions. Work indoors, outdoors, and eventually with heavier distractions present like children and other dogs.

Look into my eyes

Once your dog is reliable on these attention games, expect him to hold your gaze a little bit longer before rewarding. It's okay to use verbal encouragement. As he looks, say his name, then say in a soothing voice, 'Good boy watching me, good boy 2, good boy 3,' then give the treat. By doing this you have some way of counting how long he's held your gaze and you are also encouraging him to keep doing so. Extend this time by small increments until your dog will gaze at you for ten seconds. Always be sure when doing attention exercises that your eyes are soft and friendly, lids partially lowered, rather than hard and staring. A hard stare is a direct threat in the animal kingdom!

Try the 'Find my Face' game

Make it a bit harder for your dog to find your eyes, by turning your body slightly to the side when you call his name. He must walk around to find your face. When he does, click and treat. You may progress to facing completely away from him. Once your dog is doing wonderfully on the previous exercise, call his name as you walk away from him. Again, he must find your face to earn the treat. This is a great way to teach your dog to pay attention whether you are motionless or moving, and also sets the stage for a solid recall.

Take it on the road - now that you've got one fabulously focused dog, take your act on the road. Is there a pet shop in your area? Take your dog there. Keep the lead nice and loose and stand back a comfortable distance from the people and dogs coming and going. You don't want the distractions to be too tempting. Treat whenever your dog looks at you of his own volition. In a separate exercise, call his name, as his eyes meet yours, reward.

If you've done your homework, he may well respond to you calling his name even as another dog passes. Keep the reinforcement rate high, (treat, treat, treat!) and the game interesting. If the situation proves too distracting, don't feel badly. It just means that you need more work in lower-level distraction areas first, or at a greater distance.

Watch me

Arm yourself with plenty of treats. Find a quiet space where you can be with your dog with no distractions.

When your dog is not looking at you, maybe he is having a sniff around the floor or looking out of the window, say his name and as soon as he looks at you say, 'watch me' and hold the treat up to your face at the side of your nose, smiling.

You can talk complete drivel to him, say 'you are a lovely boy what a good boy' and say it in a high encouraging voice. He must be completely locked on to your face when you then say 'okay' and give him the treat.

If he gets distracted and looks away, do anything to get him to look at you again and start again. Do not become frustrated.

Only say 'watch me' once at the start of any time. The aim is to get to the point where as soon as you say 'watch me' your dog automatically looks up at your face.

When he is doing this well, move it to another area where there are a few little distractions and when he is doing that well, do it when you are walking your dog, or where there are a lot more distractions.

You can get other people involved in this; ask them to try and distract your dog whilst you are doing watch me.

Try for longer watches, maybe for a minute or more.

Practice out on walks, when people are going past you or there are geese or children running about.

This is a really useful 'default' behaviour to have, for instance, when there is a dog coming towards you that you know is aggressive, or people on bikes or joggers, in fact anytime you think your dog may be distracted, you can use watch me.

Sit

Most owners will figure this one out but some do struggle so here is how to do it!

Have a treat between your thumb and forefinger and show it to pup, almost putting it on the end of their nose, raise it above their head slightly and slowly so their head goes up. Aim for going over the top of their head slightly with your hand and their bum should go down. As soon as they sit, say 'sit' and feed them and tell them how great they are. Practice a few times before giving them a break.

At this point you are not asking them to sit, merely luring and guiding them into the position we want and pairing the word with the action/position once they are there.

Try to not keep repeating the command, if you keep saying sit sit sit and they are not sitting you are just teaching them how to ignore the command and besides they don't know the command properly yet either. Once pup has got the hang of being lured into the position then you can start asking for the sit before you use your hand and treat in the same way.

With practice over a couple of very short sessions you will be able to progress to not having the treat in your hand.

If you find that once you have trained this and you are asking for a sit and puppy is ignoring you, instead of asking again, use your hand in the same way as you did when you would hold a treat to train it and see if they react more/better to the visual signal and praise/reward when they do get it right.

Also consider that they may be struggling in a busy environment or where there are lots of distractions so they are struggling to focus. If they are struggling to focus try and get some space away from the distractions and practice and gradually move closer as they succeed at each step.

Please do not use the outdated method of pushing the dogs bum to the floor this can be very harmful for their hips and also their bond with you. We want them to choose to do what we ask, not be forced.

Down

Teaching the down position can be a little tricky with some pups.

Once pup has learnt to sit on command I start from this position and then again treat on nose like when we taught sit and slowly move your hand towards the floor, aiming for 1-2cm in front of their front paws. We want their nose and head to follow the treat to the ground and lower their body to try and get it too. It's rare that pup will do that first time and it's very normal for them to try and maybe nibble or paw at the treat in your fingers, keep your hand still and wait a little to see if they work it out. If pup stand up and moves around ask for the sit again and start again.

What we are wanting is bum and elbows on the floor, when this happens, say 'Down', feed them the treat and praise them. If they stay in position give them a bonus treat as this will help in future for stays and impulse control.

Just like with the sit we are just paring the word to the action at the moment. Practice up to 6 times then do something else. It won't take many sessions for you to get this in the same was that you trained the sit.

Ensure you sometimes reward just for sit, don't always follow asking for sit with down or you will end up with a pup who is convinced the word sit means down. Once they have got the idea you won't need to bother with asking for sit first as they will start to down from a stand position or do the sit first automatically.

Trouble shooting: pup won't do it? If your hand/treat is moving too fast from their nose to the floor they won't follow (also it should be a nice greasy smelly treat so they want to follow it too. Slow down your hand action and also try not to go too close or too far away from their front paws as this will encourage them to get up.

You can also reward for pup choosing to down naturally throughout the day when not asked and pair the action with the word.

Teaching the stand position

Make a stop sign with your hand and then turn it 90 degrees so it's a sideways stop sign (hand flat). Tuck a tasty treat into the crease of your thumb and encourage your puppy to follow the treat. They should be able to lick the treat but not take it until you release it.

This hand signal will be your cue to the dog to stand (without

143

using treats) once you have taught this exercise.

If puppy is in a down position slowly encouraging them to follow your hand with the treat into the stand position means you need to make a diagonal line movement from their nose in the down position up and forward a little, so they push all four paws up and allowing them to stand. Once they are in the stand position with their nose to your hand/treat, say 'stand' and release the treat.

If puppy is starting from the sit position, then as from the down position place your hand with treat just in front of their nose and this time move your hand in a straight line away from their nose so they follow it and reward when they are in this position.

Tips to keep the position for longer

- Gently scratch their shoulder blades when in the stand position.
- Talk to them and withhold the treat for a little longer before releasing each time.

Why teach the stand?

- Particularly useful for when you are doing a quick health check.
- Great for grooming your dog and will help them when they visit the grooming salon.
- Handy for when you want to bath them or dry them off with a towel.
- Very useful at the vets. Vets will often take their temperature by using a thermometer up their bum! The last thing you want is for them to sit down at this point!

The wait

The wait exercise is a very important one and can be used for a lot of different things – for instance, you can ask your dog to **wait** when:

- Going through any doorway/passage/upstairs
- When feeding
- At the kerb, when crossing a road
- When putting your dog in the car
- Even more important, when getting your dog **out** of the car
- Food manners, when giving a treat
- When doing a recall

If your dog knows the wait command, it will become used to looking at you for direction, and guidance.

The wait command is like the pause button on your TV remote, just hang on a second and then you can go.

Because food is the highest resource, it is a good idea to start training **WAIT** with food.

Put a titbit in your hand and make a fist. Show it to your dog. He will be able to smell the treat and will try to get it by licking, nibbling etc. he may use his paw. He may become a little frustrated. Don't say anything to him during this time. Just keep your hand where it is. Eventually he will sit back, or turn his head away. The moment he does this, say wait and then give him the treat. Repeat this, every time, withholding the reward until he turns away or sits back. Then try it with you palm open, saying wait.

If your dog goes to grab it, immediately close your fist and go back to the previous step.

Once your dog is waiting, you can try putting food on the floor in front of him and telling him to wait. You should be doing this one every day when you feed your dog!

It's good to have a ***release command/signal*** which tells your dog it's okay to eat etc. such as 'go on then', or 'okay' or 'take it'.

Once your dog is waiting for food, it is much more likely to wait when going through doorways, in the car etc.

The aim here is that pup can see the treat on your hand and it's within reach but they are choosing not to have it or take it till you give the release command. Dogs are scavengers by nature so it's in their natural makeup to just go in and get it, but teaching this we are showing them the best way to get what they want is to chill out, sit back and good things come to those who wait.

If your dog has a rock solid wait, all your other training will fall into place.

When you say WAIT to your dog you are effectively saying 'hang on a minute until I tell you what to do' and then you are going to tell your dog to move, to eat his food, to cross the road, to go through a door, jump in or out of the car etc.

Puppy recalls/round robin recall

To play the game you need at least 2 people, and several it's great. Each person is given a handful of very small soft treats. I prefer tiny pieces of sausage, chicken or cheese. Pieces should be VERY small, even for a larger dog or puppy. Give everyone a big handful of the treats. Once people have their treats, they should take a seat around the room with as much room between them as the room will allow.

One person takes the puppy or dog and points him towards the person who is going to begin the game. This person may do anything to get the puppy to come towards him *except* say the word COME. Clap hands, smile, laugh, show the treat, call PUPPPY PUPPPPY PUPPPPY, or the dog's name. When it is CLEAR that the pup is committed to going to the person, and ONLY THEN, say the pup's name, and **come.**

For example, Bentley, COME! It does not matter if the puppy is almost to you, as long as the pup hears his name and the word COME while he is going TOWARDS the person calling. Hold the hand with the food right up next to your body so that the puppy has to come all the way up to you and touch you to get the treat. Do not feed the treat until you are holding the puppy's collar. This prevents the 'snatch and run' game.

Praise and pet the puppy around the collar area cheerfully while he is getting his treat. Once the pup has had his little, tiny treat, it's time to point him towards another person who does the same thing.

It is extremely important that the participants understand they are NOT to say the word COME unless the puppy is already doing just that. Play as long as the pup is interested. Main rules, do not say COME unless the puppy IS coming, hold the treat up CLOSE to your body, and you must be holding the collar to feed the treat. This simple game helps to build a reliable recall, and it is fun for you and your pup. Your pup will quickly learn that his name and the word come means TREAT. Each time you call the pup and reward him for coming quickly to you, you build a more ingrained and reliable response.

If you are consistent and train this game at least 2 to 3 times per week, you will have a dog who will ALWAYS come when you call it. Most owners list this as a top priority for their dogs. Here is a fun and simple way to attain this goal. Practice often! Your pup will love this game, and so will your friends.

This is an exercise that the whole family can take part in and enjoy. Also, it will mean that anyone in the family who takes the dog out for off lead walks and exercise will be able to call the dog back to them.

The leave it exercise

Like the recall, the 'Leave it' exercise can also be a life saver for your dog. Like children, dogs are apt to pick anything up that is within reach, particularly food.

Of course, if the food your dog picks up is laced with rat poison or is a cooked chicken wing this can be fatal for your dog to eat. It can be virtually guaranteed that all dogs will pick something up in their lifetime which will make us scream "No! No! Drop it!", so it is vital to have a good grasp of this command.

Some people teach the leave it commands where you are asking your dog to wait for food or a toy and then give a command like take it or okay to tell the dog that they can have it.

To my mind leave it means leave it. *Full stop. End of. You are never having it.* I like to use the wait command when I am asking my dog to wait until I give permission for him to have something, or I am going to ask him to move at some point.

Like the wait and stay, I like to have a clear difference between wait and leave it.

Look at it this way - if you teach leave it when you are asking your dog to wait until you give your permission for it to eat or take a toy, then your dog will always be waiting for the next words out of your mouth i.e., take it, okay etc. to have what it wants.

So, you are in the park with your dog and your friend and you are chattering away to your friend and your dog spies a cooked chicken carcass (lots of thin bones that could puncture his gullet there) and goes to eat it. You have previously always taught him to wait for food by using leave it and then giving a release command. So, you see him go to gobble up the chicken and you shout LEAVE IT! YES, YOUR DOG WILL LEAVE IT … FOR A FEW SECONDS MAYBE but because normally after you say leave it you say 'take it' or 'okay' pretty soon after. So, you then turn to your friend to resume your chat and say 'anyway, or okay, what was I saying?' and your dog thinks you have given a release command and gobbles it up before you can get to him or even before you notice.

If you have taught your dog that leave it means LEAVE IT. END OF. FULL STOP. FINITO. YOU ARE NEVER HAVING IT, then in all likelihood, it will leave it. You can then use leave it for lots of things – wanting to go to other dogs or people, running or chasing birds, ducks etc., paying attention to anything you don't want him to, rolling in unmentionables etc.

So, here's how to do leave it – it's easy.

For this you will need 2 types of treat; a low value one that your dog is not too fussy about and something fantastic that your dog loves but doesn't have very often. For instance, let's say that the low value treat is a dog biscuit, and the high value treat is a piece of smoked sausage.

Now, put the biscuit in one hand and the sausage in the other and put the sausage hand behind your back. Offer your dog the biscuit on the flat of your hand, saying 'leave it' if he goes to take it, palm it and say 'ahh'. Try again. You are waiting for any hesitation, or turning of the head, or going into a down. As soon as your dog does this, say 'good leave', *put the hand with the biscuit in behind your back and reward with the hand holding the sausage.* For leaving the low value treat, your dog gets rewarded with a high value treat.

Then you could practice dropping things directly in front of him and saying, 'leave it.' *Remember to pick the low value treat that you are telling your dog to leave before you reward with the high value treat.*

Then, if you are out with your dog and he goes to chase a duck/jogger/cyclist/child or eat a rotting carcass (or roll in it!) you can say 'leave it', but you must ALWAYS reward for a leave, even if it is not with food, remember you can always use praise.

Remember leaving something could save your dog's life.

Puppy stays

This is a really useful training tip as it can be used in a whole host of situations, from stopping your dog from crossing a road to getting them to settle in their bed. You need to be very consistent when training the stay and very particular about your body language and tone of voice.

Focus on keeping your puppy calm and relaxed, so take your puppy out for a good walk first. When training the stay remain very low key, don't repeat the commands or shout them at your dog. A firm tone of voice for the 'stay' is required but a low key 'good' will reduce the likelihood of your dog coming over for its treat.

Ask your dog to either sit or down (it's up to you) and stand in front of your puppy. Make sure you have an upright posture (most people bend over when calling the dog, so don't send mixed signals). Don't have any treats in your hands, keep them in your pocket for now and make sure your puppy knows this.

Giving the cue

Give the dog the command **'stay'** with a flat palm facing the dog. Keep one foot in place and step back with the other. As quickly as you moved that foot away, take it straight back and use the sequence **'stay', 'good',** and reward. Do not try to move away too quickly or you will undo all your efforts. Once your puppy remains sat or lay still when you move your foot away, you can now take one step back with both feet. Once again return immediately and 'stay', 'good', and reward.

TOP TIP: do not use your puppy's name when training the stay or they will think you are calling them to you.

TOP TIP: when returning to your puppy don't make too much of a fuss or they will break the position they are in. A simple low key good is all that is required. Let the treat do the talking not you!

You can then start moving further and further away as your puppy remains in the same spot. This time stay away and count to three and return, slowly but surely building this up to at least 20 seconds before you create a greater distance between you and your dog.

TOP TIP: if your puppy gets up and moves during any of this training then you must say 'no' gently and patiently take them back to the exact spot they moved from, without exception.

There are 4 key initial elements to stay – distance, direction, duration and distraction.

Distance is how far away you are going to go from your dog. Initially only move one step away and increase gradually. Remember that up to now, we have been asking our dog to stay nearby, as in heel work etc. he is likely to want to go with you, so only go one step.

Direction is where you are going in relation to your dog. Always leave in the direction he is facing so that he can see you.

Duration is the length of time you are away from your dog. When starting to teach the stay it is *very important* that you only go away for a few seconds and then gradually increase the time.

Now you are increasing the distance, wait a bit longer before you go back and reward, gradually increasing the distance and duration of the stay. Do not look at your dog with a stern look on your face while you are saying 'stay' – we don't want your dog to think that he is being told off. If he does think he is in the naughty corner, then he will become anxious and will break his position. Smile and be relaxed. If your dog moves just go back and put him in the same position in the same place and start again.

Distraction - finally, we start to introduce distractions. This might start with you making a silly noise, or hopping on one leg. Silly, strange things that you won't have done while training the stay so far. I've often had owners doing star jumps as a distraction. Build up the distraction slowly and reward well. You can then build up to being able to sweep up or mop up while they are in the stay, cut up some treats on the side or play with the kids.

Getting puppy used to being groomed

Getting pup used to being groomed is very important, even when you have a dog with short fur. All dogs need an amount of grooming, whether it's the occasional bath, nail trim or a full brush through every day, never mind trips to the grooming salon for many breeds and mixed breeds.

The best time to start practicing grooming is before they are matted or 'need' grooming.

The sensation of the brush or comb against their fur and skin will feel strange at first to them and often pups will try and bite or mouth the brush.

Start with a soft brush and run it over their body when they are relaxed and tired. Do this gently. The aim isn't to groom them, merely ensure they have a positive and relaxing experience associated with this new sensation. Initially just run it down their sides and back, calm praise as they relax into it. You can also use a rubber style grooming glove or chammy leather mitt in place of a brush if you prefer. Just do this for around a minute before stopping and trying again another time or the next day.

Once pup is enjoying this level of grooming then you can slowly and gently start to progress running it over their legs, chest, ears and tail.

If you find that puppy is very resistant to the grooming item against them try any or all of the following:

- Remember that the aim isn't to brush through their fur at the moment, go very gently and slow with plenty of calm reassuring praise.
- Keep the sessions short and when puppy is tired and relaxing with you.
- Try not to get annoyed with them if they wriggle, patience and practice.
- You can use a lickimat or filled Kong or chew to keep them occupied as you work on this.
- Having a chew or activity for them will lessen their need to bite or mouth at the brush or mitt and also help to ensure they are having a positive experience.

The key areas that will get matted and can be very sensitive on longer coated breeds are at the top of the front legs, in the crease just behind their ears, the part just at the front of the top of their back legs, their legs, around the bum area and their tail. If your pup will have long hair around their muzzle and face, then these areas will need special attention too.

Slowly building up the amount of time you are grooming them and also ensuring you can groom the trickier areas is so important to ensure a happy healthy and confident dog at the groomers.

Once you are confident that puppy is accepting all areas to be groomed with something soft then look at the equipment that is recommended for your pup's coat type. This could be a slicker brush and comb or a rubber curry comb for most short, coated breeds.

For shorter coated breeds it's important that they are used to the sensation too, grooming them will help remove any dead coat and keep their skin and coat shiny and healthy.

Introduce the new grooming equipment gradually and slowly increase the pressure till you are brushing and combing through the coat properly.

It's great practice to get your dog used to the hair dryer too. If you use a hairdryer on your own hair, then allow puppy into the same room with you when you are drying your own hair, so they get used to the sound of it. At this point you are not going to blow the hot air on them, it's just so they feel confident around this strange and loud piece of equipment. After a few times of doing this, just gently wave the hair dryer past them, ensuring the hot air passed them gently and briefly and from a good distance away.

Ensure the heat is on low and almost as if you did it by accident.

Do not corner puppy or hold puppy, it just gets a gentle warm breeze for a split second.

Slowly, over a number of days build up the time that the warm air is toward their direction, reward often and praise. As you work closer to them, try not to blow the air directly into their face, instead aiming for their back end or over their back initially. Take great care with the heat and also try and avoid blowing it into their ears.

This is helpful for when puppy has their first visit to the grooming salon as they will be dried with the dog grooming equivalent to a hair dryer.

It also speeds things up for you when you may need to bath puppy and want them warm and dry quicker.

Going to the vets - pets just know!

The vets can be a scary place, there are lots of strange chemical smells, people in strange clothing and these people want to touch, handle and hold areas of your puppy that will feel very strange. They know it's not the normal loving strokes like what they get from you. Most puppies will be placed on the table for examination too. Imagine being put on the top of a high rise building with no warning and then being prodded and poked by a stranger... this is how a puppy feels at the vets for the first time, but you can help them avoid the fear and confusion beforehand and you can be armed with lots of amazing treats to help them feel more confident and enjoy this new experience.

Look at any trip to the vet to be a training opportunity, look for any chance you can for it to be a fun place to be.

Help them realise the vet is a friend!

Dogs have an amazing sense of smell; they will also smell the stress pheromones of sick and injured and stressed dogs that are there. We can't change this, but we can help to reassure our puppy that all is well.

We hope that our dogs will never get sick or injured but the chances are they will at some time in their life and that they won't be feeling great when they visit the vets.

Get vet prepped & learn how to do a daily health check

When puppy is relaxed and tired with you at home, on your lap or on the sofa (if you want them to be allowed on the sofa) gently run your fingers down their legs, to their paws. Fiddle gently between their pads and toes from above and below. Gently lift their tail slightly, run your hand along the length of their tail from base to tip.

Running your fingers and hands gently over every part of their body regularly will help them know that this is a nice relaxing experience. You can talk to them in a soothing calm voice telling them how good they are and if they decide to wriggle slightly don't worry, remove your hands and reassure them until they settle again.

It's important that with a young puppy you keep these sessions short and positive and calm.

Picking them up - safely and positively.

No matter the size or breed of your pup when they first start going to the vets, they will be small enough to be lifted onto the table for examination and there will be times that you will lift them in and out of the car etc. We do not want puppy to panic and wriggle out of your arms and fall and injure themselves.

What is the best way to pick up a dog or puppy?

Use one hand/arm to lift them from under their chest, just behind the front legs, and using your other hand/arm to gently scoop up their back end folding their back legs under them.

Try to avoid lifting them like you would a child or baby. Using both hands around their chest just under their 'armpits' and not supporting their back end can cause injury to their shoulders as all of their weight will not be suspended from here. Knowing how to pick your dog up correctly will help minimize their resistance.

Lift them slightly off the floor, maybe a foot off the floor then places them back down and reward.

If your puppy is small enough to be currently supported at both their front and back end with just one arm its great practice to feed them when they are in your arms or if they are too big for this ask someone else to feed them when they are in your arms.

It's common for many puppies to learn that being picked up is not a good thing, maybe due to being picked up to be removed from the sofa or away from something that puppy wants but is not allowed. Some puppies learn to snarl and growl at being lifted if you don't train them to enjoy it, so this is an important and simple thing to work on with them.

Picking up paws

If you teach your puppy to accept you picking up a paw/leg it will make your life so much easier as you will need to do this for many things.

This helps if you want to towel their feet dry, to check for any injury, to check for the sneaky grass seeds and burrs that love to hide in there especially if you have a pup with fluffy feet, it will help when at the vets and also allowing you to trim their nails.

The key thing to remember is to always lift a paw/leg gently and in toward their body wherever possible and within their normal range of movement to avoid causing injury, especially to a puppy whose skeleton is still very soft and can easily be damaged.

Start by gently lifting the leg slightly, not trying to do anything more than taking the weight off that leg and allowing puppy to adjust their balance when stood. Praise them and reward them with a tasty treat, repeat three times on each leg. You may find that they are more reluctant to relax when you have a front leg rather than a rear. Remember to be gentle and build this slowly. It's like someone holding your hand, restraining you and you are not able to use that whole arm, you may panic initially.

Smelling your pup's ears

This will sound strange but getting your dog used to you smelling their ears is a great thing to do! Ear infections are very common in dogs and one way we can tell is by a change in smell. Us putting our head in a dog's face to be able to do this can be quite an intimidating and threatening gesture in dog language so getting them used to this is a brilliant thing to do.

As always, practice makes perfect and encouraging and rewarding puppy for accepting you doing this regularly is important.

Knowing what is normal for your pup is key, ear infections will often come with a sweaty damp smell. Always check the colour of the inside of your dog's ears too, not only checking for ear wax but knowing what their normal skin colour is and also if you can see redness or feel heat in their ears more than normal this all points toward a possible issue and a vet's visit is needed. It's always best to catch these things earlier rather than later to ensure our pup isn't uncomfortable for long and allow for a quicker remedy and recovery.

Teeth check

Puppy will be teething from 12 weeks to around 6 months. This means they will have sore gums at times and maybe reluctant to open their mouth for inspection so keep this in mind and go gentle.

Gently just raising their upper lip to have a look at their teeth briefly then rewarding, really helps puppy to trust you with this to start with.

If we start by putting fingers in their mouths and opening their jaw, we may inadvertently cause them pain while they are teething, and we don't want them to associate us checking their teeth with pain.

Take note of the colour of their gums and inside of their lips, each dog will be different for this, there may be a mottled colouring effect and this is ok it's what may be normal for your puppy. It's useful to know what the normal colour is so if it changes, you know that there is something wrong. A change in colour can be a sign of shock. Once pup is accepting this happily, use your fingertip to gently press slightly on their gum for a split second, and then remove it. What you should notice is that the colour of the gum drains briefly.

Oral healthcare

Once you have completed the handling, health check training you

157

can start to progress onto teaching them how to accept and enjoy having their teeth cleaned. I would start without brush or any teeth cleaning equipment. Purchase some meat flavoured doggy toothpaste.

DO NOT use human toothpaste as this is toxic to your dog.

Gently offer a little of the toothpaste on your finger and see if they will lick it, it's important they like the taste to build a positive association with having their teeth cleaned.
If they like it then lift a lip and gently rub it onto one or two teeth gently then remove your finger, reward them with a tasty treat and then repeat a few times before taking a break.

At this stage you are using your finger as the toothbrush. Over the period of a few days gradually build up being able to touch more teeth but always gently.

Keep in mind that puppy may have sore gums due to teething and if you find they are suddenly reluctant I would stop and leave it for a week before returning back to training this.

After training with a finger then progress onto the rubber thimble type brushes that fit over your fingertip and once, they are confident with this it's only at this stage I would progress onto a doggy toothbrush.

It's important not to rush this training, take your time and aim for being at the final stage at around 6-7months of age.

While they are teething some things that will help soothe their gums are:

- Frozen filled Kongs
- An old face cloth with a knot tied in the middle, soaked in water or doggy gravy then given to them frozen
- Raw refrigerated carrots
- Cold watermelon slices

Take it and give/drop

There will be times during your life with your dog when you will have to take something out of his mouth, or take something off him. He may have picked up something which could be dangerous to him, or he may have something stuck in his mouth. Your dog must be ok with you being able to open his mouth and take something away.

Arm yourself with plenty of treats. Pick a toy that you dog likes but not one that he loves.

Invite your dog to play with it, saying 'take it'.

Let him play with the toy for a few seconds then take out a treat and as you hold it out to your dog he will almost certainly drop the toy to take the treat.

As soon as he drops the toy say 'give' and give him the treat. Keep repeating this over and over.

Eventually when he has done it repeatedly 10 times as he is playing with the toy, say 'give' and he should drop the toy and you can give him a treat.

Alternatively you can exchange the toy for one he likes even more, instead of the treat. Your dog will then learn that if he gives something up to you, he then gets rewarded, so it is in his interests to give it up. ***Remember: dogs are all about what's in it for them.***

You can also use food for this. Take a chew bone and hold one end of it. Offer it to your dog saying 'take it' but make sure that you hold on to the end while he is chewing it.

After a few seconds say 'give' and offer him a treat. Immediately offer him the chew again and hold it while he is chewing it. Then say 'give' and give him the treat. Repeat 10 times. Then offer the chew saying 'take it' but let go of it and after a few seconds say 'give' and as soon as he does say 'good boy' and give him the treat.

You should practice this regularly with your dog with different items.

Remember dogs value things differently just like we do; for instance I would love to eat a big cream cake a lot more than I would a boring plain biscuit, so I would be prepared to give the biscuit up a lot quicker than the cake. It's the same with dogs; your dog is not likely to want to give up a juicy lamb bone (uncooked of course!) for a bit of a bonio biscuit!

Go to bed – Race!

Key thing to remember - sending to bed should be a fun thing that they want to do, that they find fun, it should NEVER be in disgrace or when you are annoyed at them. If you have done this before, and sent them to bed as a punishment, don't panic but please don't do this in future. You can help them learn that this is new by purchasing a new bed for this exercise and by ensuring you have a very jovial and fun voice when training this game. It is a game to the dog after all!

Step 1 - standing just in front of your dogs' bed, throw a treat on the bed saying, 'on your bed' (or similar) let the dog go to get the treat on the bed, repeat 6 times.

Step 2 - repeat step 1 but ask your dog to sit or down once they have got the treat (getting them to sit/down on the bed) and reward them again while they are still in the position you have asked for – repeat 6 times

Step 3 - pretend to throw the treat on the bed (your hand doing this will become a cue to your dog as to what you expect them to do and you are kind of tricking them into thinking you have thrown the treat on there) as they surge forward to find the imaginary treat ask them to sit/down and then reward them but with two treats – so they are getting paid the same amount as before just in one go this time. Repeat 4 times.

Step 4 - introduce them staying there - after practicing the routine from step 3, ask them to stay and rock your weight backward slightly, if they stay in position and on the bed then rock toward them and reward them for staying in place. Repeat 6 times gradually being able to move away further (only by a step or two each time), returning to them and rewarding them on the bed each time.

*Trouble shooting - if your dog is being a fidget or moving off the bed when you move away or without you releasing them then slow down, don't go as far, make it easier for the dog and give lots of rewards before slowly making it harder for them again – remember to set them up for success!

I would leave the first session working on this at step 4 then revisit another time.

When you practice later the same day or another day revisit step 4 and practice 3 times before progressing onto the next step.

Step 5 - build up the distance they travel to get to their bed – the key here is to get the dog to move toward their bed ahead of you, so you do not have to follow them all of the way to their bed. Stand a couple of paces away from the bed with your dog and use your hand (as you did before, almost pretending to throw a treat) by moving it toward the bed and say 'on your bed' your dog should leave your side to go to the bed and start to sit/down automatically now if you have got the previous steps right. Rush toward them praise them and give them a treat or two telling them how good they are! Repeat at the same distance a couple of times and then step a little further away.

*Do not call them off their bed to reward them – always go to them and reward them in the position you have trained while they are still on their bed.

Build this up gradually till you can do it from another room or from the garden etc.

Remember massive rewards, and even more for when they have had to work harder and got it right (i.e. gone further to their bed than before).

*Trouble shooting – if you are finding that you have to follow your dog to their bed to encourage them to go there you have gone too far too fast. Go back to a shorter distance that you know they can do it from without you needing to follow them. Initially, you may need to move your body forward or take one step forward to encourage them to go to their bed and this is absolutely fine – as long as they go the rest of their way on their own.

If you have to keep repeating the command to go to bed then they are not fully understanding what is asked of them, try and only ask once and again go back a few steps to make it easier again for them before progressing again through the following steps.

Step 6 - keep going working on increasing both distance and the time they stay there, break it down and only work on one thing (distance or time) each time, don't increase the distance and time at the same time, as this will set your dog up to fail.

You can also apply this to their crate and places on walks too, sending your dog to a tree across the other side of a field, to a cone or place their lead or your coat on the floor and ask them to go to that.

It's also worth noting that just 10 minutes of training tires the dog mentally just as much as an hours walk! That's not to say it should replace their walk, however it's another thing you can do to get their brains working and to tire them further.

Stop your dog being a jerk – loose lead training

What are you doing? How can you change your actions?

It's funny that I find this is usually the hardest bit to learn, us people are stubborn and get into bad habits.

Ok, I'm not sure you are going to like me saying this but I can pretty much guarantee if your dog is being a jerk so are you! AND you HAVE TRAINED YOUR DOG TO PULL! (shock horror yes, I really just said that.... but stay with me and all will make sense).

Dogs will only do what works, and if you are still walking when they pull... it works! They pull you and they get to go to the park, to the field or to that blade of grass that is so amazing they must sniff at for what feels like a lifetime.

If you are jerking or pulling back on that lead you are if anything making the issue worse. Now don't get me wrong – if you simply stopped pulling them back that's not going to fix the issue but it will help your dog see you in a better light.

If I was to grab the back of your jumper and pull you back, I bet you would pull forward against it and be at least a little annoyed, wouldn't you? Think about that collar and lead, exactly the same!

Now I bet you are thinking 'well how does that help me?? I can't just run/sprint behind my dog till there's a loose lead'... that's very true.

I have been there, before becoming a dog trainer I was the biggest jerk out there, it hurts when they pull that hard and you get to the point where you feel that's the only way to go even if it just provides a millisecond of relief to your sore arm, shoulder, back, wrist... and I have tendonitis in both of my wrists so I really do 'get it'.

I was the biggest jerk till I learned how to look at it from the dog's perspective. I know there are walks when you come back and think thank god that's over for another day, and it's such a shame because your dog is so lovely in so many other ways.

I'm guessing you have pulled your dog back probably what, thousands of times? And your dog is still pulling... so it's not working is it?

STOP PULLING BACK!

Getting paid!

With our dogs, several factors influence their learning. At the simplest level though, we can say that our dogs do things for us either because they want to avoid something, or because there is something in it for them, as in show me the money!

Getting a dog to do what we ask can seem difficult at times because a dog comes with predisposed motivations provided by Mother Nature that compete with our requests. Mother Nature can be worth a lot of money to a dog – hmmmmmm, chasing a squirrel, that's worth about £20,000, affection from you, well that's worth about £3. if you are competing with Mother Nature, (squirrels, chasing joggers, eating or rolling in a dead hedgehog, playing with another dog etc.), you will need some motivation of your own. That can mean really great food treats.

Motivating your dog

When you first start training your dog, what happens when you yell 'sit!' just as a squirrel runs across your garden? Who's worth more? The £20,000 squirrel or you? At that moment in time, chasing the squirrel is a huge payoff for your dog and your shout of 'Sit!' is worthless, and if you keep repeating the word 'sit' the word loses its power. If the next door neighbour's female dog is in season and your intact male hears you yelling 'Come!' as he jumps over the fence, where's the £20,000? It's with the female dog, of course.

Chasing squirrels, barking at the postman, chasing joggers or people on bikes, meeting other dogs and rolling in unmentionables are all powerful motivators that distract your dog's attention from what you are asking him to do. In these situations, you, the erstwhile provider of all things good in your dog's universe, have taken a back seat.

Therefore, in order to get your dog to do what you want, *you* need to become worth more than the distractions. You want to elevate yourself in your dog's eyes to the position of prime motivator, so no matter what, *you're it.* You do this by controlling access to everything your dog wants. That means your dog must earn everything he wants, including food, toys and freedom.

The hierarchy of rewards

Dogs have different likes or dislikes. In human terms, think of a Las Vegas slot machine, the lottery, or horse racing. In all of these cases there are great rewards, good rewards and average rewards. In the dog's Las Vegas mentality, one dog might consider a piece of liver cake as a £10,000 reward, while another dog, at times, might consider a squeaky toy to be the highest reward possible. You need to identify what your dog values most. With some, chicken, cheese, liver etc. will do nicely. With others, they might give their all for the ball on the end of the rope, a tugger, or squeaky. Use whatever works for your dog.

As I mentioned before, rewards have a pecking order. Some are great, some good and some just okay. To keep your dog highly motivated, especially when teaching a new exercise or behaviour, always use great rewards, ones that are worth £10,000 in human terms.

To my mind, a great treat bag would have 3 different high value (things your dog really loves) treats, for instance, chicken, liver and garlic cake, sausage, and mild cheese (cuts up better and doesn't crumble). Your dog is not going to know which morsel of food is coming next and will keep motivated for the whole session. The opposite treat bag to this, a rubbish treat bag, would be bits of smackos, gravy bones, or even worse, bits of crunchy bonio.

Different dogs will value some treats over others - just like we do, I know I like chocolate, but if you offered me cake I'd be in heaven. I once trained a lovely fox terrier and he valued strawberries over anything, even liver!

Think how your dog feels when he's performed a new behaviour brilliantly and you reward him with *ta – da!* – a boring bit of biscuit. Why should he do that brilliant behaviour again for you? He will lose interest and motivation, as you would – imagine you are at work and your boss asks you to take on a new project. You don't know anything about it but nevertheless, you throw yourself into it, do lots of research, stay at work late a few nights, go in early, and eventually you finish it. You are really proud of what you have achieved and you present it to your boss, with eager anticipation. He picks it up, glances quickly at it and says, 'Yeah, that'll do I suppose, now can you make me a coffee?' how would you feel? But more importantly, if he asks you to do another special project what would you say?

So think about what's in your treat bag, or pocket and if there are just crumbly bits of biscuit in there, do the same session with a bulging bag of £10,000 titbits and just see the difference it will make.

Going back to rewards, rewards have to *keep* their value. If the same great reward is given over and over again, it will lose its value. Other rewards, such as praise, can also be misused and lose their power.

Of course, you want to praise your dog consistently for doing what you have asked. But if you give him praise for doing nothing, he may begin to ignore you.

Rewards – to be rewards – have to keep their value. If your dog has done something spectacular, for example, you may have been trying to train the stay for ages, but he always gets up in the last 10 seconds, but this time he stayed rock solid, then give a jackpot reward, (quietly, while he is still in the stay position) £50,000 worth.

Of course, you can cheat a little and occasionally give a £10,000 treat just for the hell of it, because he's such a great dog and you're just a wonderful person!

It's always best to buy a new harness/collar and lead so you can start from scratch building a new set of rules in the dog's mind that things are different now.

Only put on the new equipment when you are going to be training so you can set yourself and the dog up for success.

This is the part with my one to one training clients that I get the big sigh and the eye roll!

'Urgh! More leads! I have a box full, and none have worked!'

Yep, I'm sure they have and likely you have your own collection too, but I'll let you into a little secret as to why.

Because walking nicely on lead is all about the bond you have with your dog and how interesting and fun you are, and equipment is only a fraction of this!

Us humans are always after a quick fix.

We have busy lifestyles and spending a few pounds on some new cleverly marketed gadget gives us hope that all our problems will be solved. Repeat this a few times and we just give up hope of ever training the dog to stop pulling and resign ourselves to being dragged everywhere for years to come.

Why doesn't it work? Well usually (if you are lucky) it works for a few walks and then gradually the dog learns how to pull against it, and we carry on walking so the dog learns again that pulling works, even if the dog is uncomfortable.

How can we change this?

By actively rewarding them when they are being good and not pulling on the new equipment, and keeping up the regular rewards over many walks until you can phase them out, and the dog is clear that not pulling is more rewarding than pulling. When your dog puts any pressure on the new equipment/gadget/lead we must stop walking forward, to make it even clearer to the dog that pulling does not work.

We are going to stop saying anything that means walk nicely, this could be 'heel' 'walk' 'steady' 'close'. Usually all this means to the dog is 'brace yourself you're going to get yanked!' I'm betting you have never properly taught them what 'heel' means (i.e. walk nicely by my side), instead up to this point you have said 'heel' and then pulled them back.

We are not going to have a verbal command or word for walking nicely. Instead the equipment being placed on the dog will be the command.

Eh?

Think about guide dogs for the blind. When their yellow vest is put on when they leave the house, their owner doesn't have a conversation with them about what they are expected to do when they are out and about, instead it's the vest that is the signal to the dog to say what is expected of them, and we are going to train our dogs in the same way.

We are going to teach our dogs that the rules are always the same when the lead is attached, which means some self-control and consistency from us as much as them!

The lead I would recommend is the Halti Training Lead it's padded which makes it a lot easier on your hands, durable and has many uses with its adjustable length and double clip features.

Harnesses I would recommend are a two point, fully adjustable Y shaped front harness (Perfect Fit, Ruffwear, Hurtta and Puppy Love are just a few brands who have this style of harness).

Following on from not telling our dogs to 'heel' 'walk' etc.

Stay silent when you pick the lead up - NO 'WALKIES!'' 'Wanna go for a walk?' etc. If they are dancing around getting excited for the walk, put it back down make a cup of tea, do something else before trying again. The lead only goes on when your pooch is calm or sitting (if they are excited at the prospect of a walk and they are still in our world, our home…this is only going to be turned up at least 5 notches when we enter their world. The great outdoors and the battle is already lost.

Put more importance on talking to them positively and rewarding them for walking nicely on a loose lead rather than concentrating on correcting them pulling.

Give 5 to 10 treats for being by your side before you even take a step forward once the lead is attached and feed them when they are next to you, this is to be clear to the dog that being calm and by your leg is what you want.

Every time they pull you out of the door, you go back into the house (with the dog) and do something else before trying again…a nice calm exit from the house is the start of a good walk and its good manners.

Reward them for being next to you on a loose lead with stinky treats or a stroke and a 'good dog' regularly when on the move.

Reward them when they are next to you, don't feed them when they are in front of you. If you always feed from next to your leg, they will want to stay in that area because it pays to be there!

Only talk to your dog when you need their attention (as above) or to say good dog if you manage to even get one pace of loose lead walking …in other words, no saying heel, close, with me etc., no command for this.

In these early stages of training try to stay at a distance from other dogs or people that your dog may want to pull to, we want to set them up for success and make this as easy as possible for both you and the dog.

Never, ever take another step forward when there is pressure on the lead… if they are pulling to the end of it simply turn and walk in the other direction while encouraging them to follow or walk backwards (if it's safe to do so) or call them to you before proceeding forward.

Any amount of pressure on the lead from either you or the dog should always result in you stopping and doing something else to encourage the dog to take a loose lead before you continue.

Don't be a jerk, don't yank the lead back, if they lunge forward or sideways just use their name in a happy tone (even if it's through gritted teeth) and give them a little treat if they just look back at you… the more you practice this the quicker they will come back to you and the less they will do it in the first place… as long as you follow the other steps.

Don't do your normal walk route and let them off lead after pulling, change your route and direction often.

If you have got this far, now is the time to throw away that flexi lead (extendable lead) or at least stop using it for walks on pavements.

Why? Because your dog will never learn to walk on loose lead whilst ever you are using one for 'lead walking', using it on the park because you don't trust your dog off lead is another matter (and email training course) altogether!

Now we are going to look at what you are doing, how you hold the lead and what your body language is saying to the dog.

The wrong things to do
- Walk along either looking at your dog or at the floor
- Wind the lead around your hand – AKA the Death Grip
- Hold the lead by the handle, hand by your side
- Walk along looking at or talking on your phone
- Always take them to the same area to let them off lead and let them off at the gate/entrance to the field or park or path
- Go on a walk with the dog when we are annoyed, frustrated, over tired or just simply had a bad day
- Give up training, especially at any point whilst on a walk (so the walk finishes with the dog pulling)
- Expect the dog to have been trained after a couple of days/sessions

The right things to do
- Walk tall, with your head held high, shoulders back

Why? Because if we aren't looking ahead, our dog needs to feel safe, and will do this by 'being on lookout' constantly looking for anything in the distance which in turn makes him more likely to be in front and pulling. Walk your dog like you drive a car – look at the furthest point. You can see your dog out of your peripheral vision (and you can feel if your dog puts pressure on the lead with your lead hand). You can also see anything else that your dog may be excited by, by looking ahead.

- Hold the lead with one hand, leaving the other able to dispense treats for nice walking. Your lead hand should not be the hand nearest the dog.

What? How does that make sense?

If your dog is on the left hand side for example, your lead should be held with your right hand and kept on your belly button, this gives you more strength if your dog decides to lunge suddenly as keeping your limbs into your body gives you more stability and balance when pulled.

- Have a rule that your mobile only comes out on a walk to take pictures of your dog.

If we walk along on our phones our dogs know we have 'switched off' and will revert back to pulling, we will have often taken ten steps with them pulling before we stop and realise, which has just rewarded pulling again.

- Only go on a walk when we are in the right frame of mind.

Never leave the house with the dog if you are already in a bad mood, sit down have a cup of tea, relax and chill out before setting off on a walk. Our dogs know us very well and often when we are in a foul mood they react by behaving badly which then creates a viscous cycle and the walk isn't fun or relaxing in any way.

Hungry for more tips?

Shorter training sessions are easier on both you and the dog, remember both human and dog only have a limited amount of concentration and patience. A week of shorter walks resulting in better lead walking will allow them more freedom in the long run so don't beat yourself up for the dog not getting as much exercise in the short term. The ideal training walk in the first week would be 5-

10 minutes long at least twice a day. This may be the only exercise they get that day, that's ok! Remember this is short term. If you still want to take them for an off lead run, my best advice would be to drive them to somewhere they can have a run. Take your old lead (previous to training) in case they need to be put on lead around other dogs etc. or a flexi or longline if they are not reliable when off lead.

Getting it right for short distances is key. If we don't have the foundations right we can't expect them to do it for longer distances. Initially this may be just up and down your garden path or 20 yards up and down your street (backwards and forwards). Provided you can get shorter distances right you can start to double the distance, then triple etc.

Once you get to the point where you can get to the park/field that they usually get to go off lead, do a few days of walking to it and simply walking back home again without them getting to go off lead at that point. This helps to reduce the excitement and likelihood of pulling you to the gateway or place they usually get freedom.

If you have done this for a few days and want to them let them off lead at this point, only let them off lead after a good 10 steps of loose lead walking past the point where you would usually let them off and ask for a sit and wait as you unclip the lead before verbally releasing them. Over time you can build the distance past the gateway and the time you ask them to wait once the lead is removed.

High quality smelly treats will be needed a lot in the initial stages, you may need to reduce their daily food allowance to compensate and avoid them gaining weight. You will not need the same amount of treats forever and you will in time be able to phase these out altogether and just keeping up with the odd 'good dog' verbal praise, provided you get the foundations correct.

You will need to practice the training in lots of different environments before you can simply take them anywhere and expect the same loose lead walking. A high street or busy park will be a more exciting place for your dog than round the block at home so you may need to up the rewards in busier environments for a while.

Personally I never expect my dogs to be glued to my heel when on a walk, as long as they are not putting tension on the lead and not crossing in front or behind me, I'm happy. You may have different rules and ideas on what you want or where you want your dog to be, and that's perfectly fine, just remember to concentrate on rewards when they are where you want them to be.

If you have a very strong dog who can pull you off balance when you stop still, always stand with your feet shoulder width apart. Keep your lead hand on your core/bellybutton. Or stand on the lead whenever you stop, particularly if you are stopping to talk to someone. The more your dog gets the chance to pull you off balance and you take that extra step to get your balance back, the more they will do it because it worked. Practicing just these few things will give you a lot more balance and strength and help prevent them to even try to do this in future because it doesn't work anymore.

You now have all the tools you need to stop your dog being a jerk!

Here is a quick recap:

- New equipment
- Reward for what you want the dog to do, often
- Head up, lead on bellybutton/core
- Don't pull back
- Never ever take another step when there is tension on the lead
- Short distances and short training sessions
- Practice and patience
- Make it easy for the dog (i.e. stay away from dogs and people to start with)
- Mix up your routes
- Rules apply from the second the lead goes on to the second it comes off
- No mobile phones on walks
- Only go out on walks when you and the dog are calm
- Positive mental attitude, envisage what it looks like for you and your dog to take a lovely stroll out together.
- Stand with your feet shoulder width apart and lead on

your core for better balance when pausing on walks

Now go and make it happen!

If you are like many of my clients who need me to show them rather than tell them about loose lead training, I offer a home study course that gives you everything I have ever learnt about loose lead walking and lots of videos to demonstrate all the methods for you and your dog. In just three weeks you can turn it all around you can grab it by visiting here https://www.houndhelpers.co.uk/plans-pricing, selecting the Daily drag offer. you can have it for just £33 down from £195.

Settle Training

Many young and exuberant, bouncy dogs struggle to switch off. Teaching them to settle is far from rocket science once you know how! If you really work on this then it's something that you can 'take one the road with you' and be able to ask your dog to settle in the pub, at a friend's house or in a dog friendly café etc.– really useful for if you are holidaying with your pooch!

Your dog learning to relax while you are at home, doing housework, relaxing in front of the TV and just generally mooching around at home is a very different thing to sleeping at night or when you are out of the house.

If your dog is struggling then as well as chews, interactive toys, stuffed songs, lickimats etc. we can practice 'Netflix and Settle'

Move your dog's comfy bed or blanket so its next to the sofa or chair that you relax in when washing TV or read a book or flick through social media on your phone/tablet/laptop etc.
*You could also place the bed next to your desk if you are working and practice the same thing.

Think about how your dog normally sleeps or relaxes and in what position.

What is normal for him? What does the relaxed picture look like for your dog?

Do they rest their chin on their paws, hips rocked over to one side? Do they tuck one paw under their chest? Lay flat on their side? Legs akimbo upside down? Only you will know what is normal for your dog.

Have some small, low value treats to hand. Do not have these treats in a plastic bag or something that will make a noise every time you touch them.

Dog and bed on one side of chair/sofa/desk etc. and treats on the other (ideally out of sight of the dog).

*You may need to ask for bed and down first a few times in a calm manner before being able to progress with this

As you sit and watch tv or be preoccupied in some way or another, keep a watchful eye on your dog in your peripheral vision.

Initially, quietly and sneakily drop a treat just in front of their nose every time your dog takes a step toward being relaxed and not looking at you. Ideally you should be dropping the treat through the crate, so it falls just by their mouth/nose, so they only have to make minimal movement to eat the treat.

It's important that we stay quiet (no talking to the dog) and reward the dog for NOT looking at you. This may feel quite backwards as most training we do involves the dog concentrating on us.

We want to start making incremental steps toward your dog truly relaxing and sleeping in their crate while you are 'busy' but present and in the same room. We do this by paying them at regular intervals and every time they are making steps toward that.

Your dog focusing on your every move isn't a dog in a relaxed and sleepy mind-frame. We want them to switch off. The timing of the reward, the value of the reward to your dog and you being quiet are all keys to success to this.

Consider the value of the treats you are using.

For this exercise low value treats are needed.

Too high value, or too exciting means your dog will be anticipating the next treat too much and not relax.

All dogs will value different treats differently.

Just like I prefer cake over chocolate, I also like oaty biscuits, but I would rather have cake above all.

If I were to put myself in the dog's position here biscuits would be the best thing to train... if one landed in front of me, I would be 'oh thanks, nom'

Chocolate 'ooh THANKS!'
Cake 'OMG best day ever, CAKE! Amazing thank you!!! NOM! Anymore??'

For some dogs a low value treats maybe some of their normal kibble if they are fed on dry food, or a raw piece of carrot.

Feed often for the dog choosing to get comfy, stay comfy and then get comfier. All while you are appearing to be preoccupied.

Troubleshooting: If your dog is getting either excitable or getting up, fidgeting lots etc. (assuming it's not for a toilet trip). Don't make eye contact. Stay calm, don't get frustrated at them, ask for a down on the bed and reward after they have stayed there for a short while. Have patience and wait until they do something, anything that suggests they are starting to relax or switch off then reward.

Keep these sessions short initially, 5-10 minutes and then build up the time by practicing regularly.

Recall issues

A very common issue I see and help owners with is when they

are struggling to get their dog to return to them when called. Often what they have done inadvertently is devalued their recall command by overusing it. If we keep the repeating the same command and the dog isn't paying any attention we are teaching them how to ignore it, not respond to it.

'Fido come….come….come….COME!' often turns almost into a beacon to the dog too, they can hear where you are because you are shouting yet something else is more interesting, they are confident that they won't lose you because they can hear where you are and will return when they have finished investigating that scent or chasing that rabbit, bird or playing with that dog.

A recall command needs to be sacred and only used when we are confident in the dog to return (or at least as much as is possible and practical). We also need to ensure that the dog is confident that returning to you is a great thing and that you are more fun than whatever they may be distracted by.

A whistle is a great tool to have and if trained correctly it can be the answer to all of your recall woes. I tend to steer away from the 'silent' dog whistles as I find if we can't hear it we are more likely to repeatedly keep blowing it (and in turn start to de-value the command), as our brains start to convince us that it isn't working. My favourite whistles are the ACME gundog whistles as they are widely available come in a variety of pitches/sounds, not to mention the variety of colours too if you like things to match, or maybe a bright orange one that's easy to spot on the ground if you drop it.

It's not about the sound or which pitch it is, more about how you train it and keep the use of it sacred. But once you start training with a certain pitch, take a note of what it is (the most common ones are 210.5 and 211.5) just in case you ever lose it and need to replace it. If you don't replace it with the same pitch you will likely need to start training all over again.

A great benefit to a whistle is everyone in the household can use it and its exactly the same sound no matter who uses it, (as long as you are sure they won't 'overuse' it) and no matter how annoyed you maybe at the dog at the time of blowing it, it still sounds the same.

Unlike how our voices change and convey our emotions if the dog doesn't return the first time.

The whistle command I normally use it just two short blasts (toot toot).

Week 1

Days 1-4

When your dog is sat waiting for his food just before you give the release command to eat, blow the whistle with two short blasts and then immediately give the release command('Ok' 'Take it' etc.), do this at every meal.

Days 4-7

Carry on with the above but also when calling your dog to you in and around the house, but not in from the garden yet.

When you want to give your dog attention, or to put their lead on etc. just blow the whistle in the same fashion as when feeding (two short blasts) then immediately verbally call your dog, give lots of physical praise for coming to you then hold the collar in one hand before giving a food treat.

Week 2

At this point you can stop blowing the whistle at feeding times, but continue as above around the house, introduce the same thing when calling your dog in from the garden, giving more physical praise for the correct behaviours.

Week 3 onwards

Continue using the whistle when calling in from the garden. By this point your dog should know what the whistle means, so a verbal command is now not needed. When out on a walk, start using the whistle for shorter distance recalls with no distractions such as other dogs or people. Once you have had success with this on walks for over a week, start gradually introducing the whistle for recall with distractions. Starting with a person far away, gradually building up to a person with a dog the other side of a field, and then closer and closer over the following weeks.

Notes to remember

Always set your dog up for success, not for failure – do not skip any steps. Also don't ask too much of your dog by asking them to come back from playing with a pack of dogs after only using the whistle for two or even three weeks. When the dog returns to you after blowing the whistle on a walk remember to give lots of physical praise and to vary the food treats, ham, sausage, cheese etc. or sometimes a 'jackpot' of a whole chicken breast! A game with your dog's favourite toy can work just as well.

If you do any of the following things on your walk, I'm sorry but you are being a real snooze fest for your dog!

Playing on your phone, scrolling through social media, catching up with your friends, chatting on the phone, listening to music, going on the same walks every day and or being predictable with where your dog is asked to go back on lead.

Doing any of the above really doesn't give your dog any reason to return to you, you are no fun.

Dogs do what works, what is fun and what makes them happy. Loose lead walking and recall are directly related and a measure of the bond between you and the dog. Outside, the dogs nose is on overdrive, they can smell and identify all of the people dogs and creatures that have passed that same spot over the last 6 weeks. With this in mind it may help you to understand that your dog isn't disobedient but actually gathering information when he's sniffing at yet another blade of grass. It's like the dog equivalent of social media, checking on their notifications and 'peeMail'

Go on walks with a toy they love to play with and/or smelly treats such as chicken, sausage, left-overs from your roast etc. Practice calling your dog back regularly throughout a walk – not just when you see another dog or when you get to the end of the walk. When they return give them a treat (if they came flying back, give them a handful!) and have a good play with them. If they take longer than you would like to come back, try to refrain from calling their name over and over (this becomes a background noise), give a single treat and try again next time. The worst thing you can do is tell your dog off for taking ages to come back. Although this can be frustrating, all the dog learns is that coming back results in being told off (they do not learn that ignoring you in the first place equals you being disappointed or annoyed at them). Put importance on making it fun for them to return to you. Dogs learn to read your signals as to when the lead will go on and they lose their freedom, so practicing clipping it on and off regularly throughout the walk helps this.

How can we be more fun and encourage them to return to us more?

Here are some games to play with your dog when they are off lead to increase their desire to come back to you, or stay with you when needed.

Start playing all of these games when there are no other dogs or people present so you can set your dog up for success before progressing to practicing when there are distractions present.

- 'Hide and Seek' – if your dog is a distance away, step off the track or path and hide behind a bush, tree, fence or in some long grass, maybe crouch down if needed, you can either stay quiet or call them just once and wait for them to find you. We want to encourage a little bit of panic here, and make a big fuss of them when they return and find you. You can also back this up with the smelly treats too.

- 'Look what I found' – if your dog is ahead of you and 'busy' sniffing or running, whilst they are not looking just place two or three treats in the grass near you, try to make a mental note of where you have placed them, call your dog back and when they have returned say 'find it' and use your hand to guide them to the treats, you can also replace the treats with toys or a ball if your dog is toy obsessed, when they get the treat or a toy, follow with lots of verbal praise.

- 'Follow me' – woodland areas are the best place to practice this. Turn off, taking different paths often, particularly when the dog is ahead. Don't say a word, keep walking and when they catch up with you praise and reward. This encourages them to check where you are more, to prevent you always being worried about where your dog is when off lead.

Keeping the command sacred

Interestingly, I find that dogs are even more likely to return you when called immediately after 'leaving a deposit' for you to collect and dispose of. Don't ask me why, but do I know I'm not the only trainer who has noticed this!

Try not to go over your dog's head when replacing the lead, instead clip from under the chin if you are attaching to a collar, or approach from the side if using a harness. Going over the dog's head can be a little threatening and scary to some so they may avoid coming so close to you because of this.

Squatting down on your knees (without looming over the dog) is also an encouraging gesture for the dog to come into your space.

Reward every time not only for the dog returning but also again after you have replaced the lead.

Replace the lead often and randomly throughout the walk. Sometimes clipping it on and then off again immediately, other times replacing lead, rewarding, walking for a couple of steps before releasing them again.

Consider what you are doing with the lead when it's not attached to the dog. If you always go to hold it, take it out of your pocket or unclip it from your body BEFORE calling the dog to come back to have its lead on, then this is a very obvious sign to the dog that they are about to lose their freedom, and are less likely to return to you on these occasions.

If you think you may be doing this (don't worry it's very common and you may not even be aware of this pattern) then leave the lead where it is.

Call your dog back (leave the lead alone), slip a finger in their collar or harness (again being mindful not to go over the dogs head) before releasing the treat with your other hand. This gives you the control you need so you can then use the hand you used to feed a treat to your dog to get the lead from your pocket or wherever you may have stored it. Don't forget to reward your dog again once the lead is clipped on.

Ditch the sit!

At least while you are going through the retraining process, please refrain from asking your dog to sit every time you call it back to you. Dogs only associate what they are doing in that moment or what they have done a split second before with a reward or payoff so asking them to sit is only rewarding them for the sit, not for them returning to you.

Remember that your new command for recall whether it be a whistle or a new word is precious and should not be over used.

If you are not confident that your dog will return to you in certain situations yet – playing with other dogs for example. Then do not use the whistle to call them yet! Use their name, a noise to encourage them to come. Consider how far you are away from the dog and how likely they are to follow or return to you when called.

It is so very important to only use the new command/whistle when you are over 80% sure that your dog will return.

182

If you have rushed a step or got it wrong and your dog does not return to you when using the whistle, then do something else - use your voice, squeak a toy, hide (if safe to do so) do anything to encourage the dog to return. DO NOT keep blowing the whistle!

If you keep blowing it, the dog is just learning once again how to ignore you and you are undoing all of your work in training!

Here is a recap to get a better recall:

- Choose a new command – ideally a whistle
- Train often with the whistle – don't rush it!
- Be more fun
- Play games on walks
- Set your dog up for success
- Pay your dog well for coming back to you
- Change where you put your dog back on lead on a walk
- Put your phone back in your pocket - be interactive
- Never shout at your dog for coming back to you, no matter how slow they may have been
- Finger in collar or harness before releasing the treat
- Ditch the sit

The differences between give/drop, leave it, wait and stay

In the grand scheme of things it doesn't matter. However what does matter is what your dog perceive are the rules of each game or command. This is how I teach these words:

Stay - stay there indefinitely and I will always return to you to release you. Useful for dog staying by the table at a pub while you grab the next round, go to your bed and stay. I manly use it to keep my dogs safe when I have been clumsy and dropped a glass or cup and I need to sweep/hoover/mop up the mess and I don't want their paws getting cut – I tell them to stay while I clear up and then return to each one to release them when it's safe.

Wait – hang on a second, shorter time frame, usually there is movement toward me or an item upon my release command, whether it be toward the food bowl toward me through a gate or doorway but it's usually stop go stop go.

Leave it – you are never going to get it end of, back up, don't go near and you will get rewarded. This is not to be used with toys. This could save their life. This is not for when they have already got an offending item in their mouth.

Give/drop – spit it out. Toy, treat, something you shouldn't have or something you are allowed. Sometimes you may get these items back sometimes you may not.

More training?

Training tricks – I meet lots of clients who aren't interested in training their dog to do tricks and they want to train them how to be better behaved rather than what they perceive as waste time training tricks. Remember everything we teach a dog it a game or a trick, sit is a trick so sometimes we need to look at things in a different way.

Tricks can be just cute and something to do, something to show your friends but they can also be very useful too!

It's also worth noting that just 10 minutes of training tires the dog mentally just as much as an hours walk! That's not to say it should replace their walk, however it's another thing you can do to get their brains working and to tire them further.

Rules for training and the steps I give – I may say how many times you should repeat each step – if I say 6 times, by this I mean that you should have had 6 times of success with it before moving on to the next step, if you have not had this amount of success with your dog keep going at the same step (sometimes move back a step briefly before progressing).

Use a marker word; how to get started

This is instead of Clicker training, a common form of positive reinforcement, is a simple and effective training method. The clicker is a metal strip inside a small plastic box that makes a distinct clicking sound when pressed. The click is much faster and more distinct than saying 'good dog' and much more effective than using treats alone. To teach a dog the meaning of the click, a treat is given immediately after clicking.

I often find that a clicker, treats, lead, poo bags, toys and the puppy is too much to handle at first for most pup owners and a marker word can be an amazing thing to have to speed up training to communicate with our dogs what we want quickly and efficiently.

Clicker/marker training is not meant to completely replace the use of treats. The sound of the click or word instantly tells the dog that what he has done will earn him a reward. To emphasise this, clicks/word should always be followed by treats. Otherwise, the word will lose its effectiveness... It's very important to use strong rewards a lot during initial training stages, and treats are often the strongest reward for a dog.

Firstly, we need to decide what word to use. I use the word 'Yes' but I have known others used yip, ping, pow etc. it doesn't matter but it should be something you can say easily and quickly and be just one syllable.

Here's how to you can easily train your dog to respond to the marker word before moving on to basic and advanced training

The following steps are often referred to as "charging" the marker:

- Begin with your dog in a quiet area
- Have a handful of your dog's favourite treats ready. Ideally, this should be done when your dog is hungry.
- Say the marker word and immediately give your dog a treat. Repeat 5-10 times.
- You can test your success by saying the word when your dog is not paying attention to you. If your dog responds to it by suddenly looking at you, then looking for a treat, you are ready to move on.

- Next, begin teaching your dog basic commands. At the *exact moment* your dog performs the desired action, say the word. Follow with a treat and praise.

One of the best things about the marker word is the accuracy. The dog associates his action with the word and, subsequently, the reward. Not only does he better understand what he is doing, this also makes him more likely to repeat the action when asked in the future. Marker word training can also be very effective for advanced training. You simply click for small steps toward the behaviour and work the dog toward the final, completed behaviour; this allows you to be totally hands-off (except for delivering the reward, of course). You don't need to manipulate the dog into position, which can often slow the process.

Remember:

The word equals a treat - when you say your word to mark behaviour, you must give your dog a treat. You need to teach your dog that the sound of the click is an extremely reliable predictor that he is about to get a treat. If you don't always give a treat after you click, the clicker begins to lose some of its effectiveness. You don't always have to use a marker when you train your dog, but if you say the word, you must give a treat – it's a promise to the dog that a treat is coming.

Timing is everything - it's important that you say the word at the exact moment your dog performs a behaviour. If you aren't precise with your clicker, you might end up reinforcing the wrong behaviour. For instance, if you ask your dog to sit, and he does it, you should say the word the minute his rear end hits the floor. If you wait even a few seconds too long, your dog might start getting up, and the behaviour you mark is him raising his bottom a few inches from the floor. You are not reinforcing the behaviour you want. Be sure that you are clicking to mark the exact behaviour you want.

Keep it positive - remember that training is supposed to be fun for you and your dog. If you find yourself getting frustrated, end the training sessions. You can go back later and start fresh.

Twist/Twirl

Dogs are left pawed and right pawed, much like us.

If they like to go and fetch things like a ball you may notice that they will mainly choose to twist a certain way (to the left or right) once they have reached the ball to then turn to get back to you this is because they find that way easier. Just like I'm a lefty… it's very difficult to write with my right hand! Also, just like us, dogs get aches and pains and sore muscles and of course if we are in a little bit of pain we won't be as relaxed as we could be. It's important that they stretch and use both sides of their body, a very simple way to help them do this and use both sides of their body is to teach the twist - spin around to the right and the twirl spin around to the left *It really doesn't matter what word you use; some people use spin and twist. I use twisty/twirly as twirly has an L in it, I remember that's the one to the left.

Step 1 - with your dog in the stand position put a treat to their nose, slowly (and level with their head/nose) move the treat away and start to draw a big circle with the treat for the dog to follow and encourage them to walk around in a circle. Bring them all the way back around to you so they are facing you again and give them the treat and give them a big fuss. Repeat 3 times.

*Trouble shooting:
- Your dog may auto sit when presented with you in front of them and a treat in hand. To get them into the stand simply put a treat on their nose and pull the treat slowly forward/out away from the dog's nose in a straight line so they follow it, and their back legs pop up. As soon as they have done this, feed them the treat and tell them how amazing they are. You may need to practice this a few times before progressing on to starting to teach the twist or twirl.
- You may need to use all of your body and lean over the dog to draw a big circle for larger dogs such as Labradors and German Shepherds, they need more space to walk around in a circle and your body needs to give enough space for them to do that.

- If you find your dog is not following the treat and is sitting or going into the down position when you move the treat then you are probably holding the treat too high (causing sitting) or too low (creating the down). Try and keep the treat and your hand on level with the dog's head and back all the way around the circle.
- If your dog will go so far around the circle but not all the way, don't try to go full circle, just go part way where you know they are comfortable to and reward here a few times before trying to ask them to follow your hand further.
- If your dog is struggling to go one way initially try the other way as you may find that they are better this way (again back to right pawed or left pawed. Interestingly horses are also the same). Set them up for success and make it easy to start with as this helps their confidence and will help them learn faster.

Step 2 - put a word to it and reverse it - practice 3 times more in the same direction you have had success at step 1, as they are mid spin (i.e. facing away from you on the circle) say the word you would like to use. Now practice the other way 6 times putting the other word to it mid spin.

Remember: if you have wound them around and around one way you must practice the other way as many times to unwind them, to ensure both sides are getting the same work out. You may find that they don't get it straight away when you reverse the direction, have patience and revisit the trouble shooting and step 1 – have faith, they will get it!

Step 3 - try it without a treat in your hand. Do as you did in the previous steps, pretending you are holding a treat. Use your hand to guide them and they follow as before and then give them a treat or reward from your other hand once they have done their circle. Practice 3 times in each direction.

Step 4 - make them work harder while you work less! Say the word twisty/twirly/spin etc. then pause for a second before then guiding with your hand. The key here is to ensure they are hearing the word before you move, and you gradually make a smaller circle with your hand/arm with each repetition as they have the idea now.

Repeat 5 times each way – you slowly making less movement each time.

Great work!

Wipe your feet

A useful one to teach when the garden is muddy or if your dog suffers seasonal allergies from things like pollen or grass (more common than you would think).

Start with a thin doormat; the cheap ones that you would get at the pound shop are usually a good one to train with.

Step 1 - place a tasty smelly treat underneath the corner while your dog is watching, stand on the corner or hold it down with your hand so your dog is unable to use their nose to get it. As soon as he puts his paw on it say wipe and remove the corner of the mat so your dog can take the treat – repeat 5 times.

Step 2 - now we are going to wait for your dog to do a bit more. Repeat the previous step but instead of releasing the treat for merely putting a paw or two on the mat we are going to wait for them to move their paw across the mat, no matter how small the movement, placing their paw or paws on the mat and then moving them any attempts to scratch to get the treat needs to be encouraged at this point so remove your hand and the corner of the matt so they can access the treat reward straight away. Repeat 6 times.

Step 3 - now place the treat further under the mat, more toward the middle – you may need to stand on the edges of the mat to keep it taught and prevent them trying to access the treat with their nose under the mat or even run off with the mat. Repeat 3 times.

Step 4 - repeat the previous step but wait for your dog to do more scratches before letting them get to the treat. If they were doing 2 scratches before, wait it out and see if they will do 4. At the moment all we want is a little more than before so wait it out, even if its 2 scratches, pause 2 scratches and then you reward this is great!

Repeat 5 times.

Step 5 - introduce the word. This maybe wipe, clean, muddy paws, it doesn't matter really just pick a word to use and stick with it – only say it while the dog is actually scratching at the mat (we are not asking for it yet, merely pairing the word with the action, as it is happening) add this to step 4 and practice 5 times.

Step 6 – change how you reward. While trying to wait for a little more scratching than before and instead of letting them access the treat underneath as a reward just throw a treat away from the dog and the mat and let them go and get it, this was your dog will move away, get the treat and return to you and the mat to try again. As they start to approach the mat again say the word you want to use (wipe, clean etc.). Don't repeat the word when they are doing the scratching now. Repeat this step 4 times.

Step 7 - remove the treat from underneath the mat and practice step 6 - repeat 6 times.

Remove the mat for now and put it down the next time you practice.

Step 8 - revisit step 7, you may notice your dog come to approach the mat as soon as you get it out. Practice a few times to ensure they remember and have 'got it' now wait for them to scratch, then ask for twist/spin, ask for a scratch again then throw a treat for them as a reward. Practice this new routine of scratch twist, twirl, scratch at least 6 times.

*If your dog seems to be confused as to what is expected of them when you revisit step 7, go back a step – putting the treat under the mat and I'm sure they will remember and start to progress quickly again.

Step 9 - reduce the commands/ talk less. This time you are going to ask for wipe or clean (command/word you have been using) and wait it out! See if they scratch, then spin without you asking for the spin throw 2 treats away on the floor for them (they have worked harder and worked out what you want). Repeat this until you can get all 4 tasks (scratch, twist, twirl, scratch) with just one command – every time they take a step toward what you want – massive amounts of rewards to show them you appreciate them trying hard.

Take a break put the matt away.

Step 10 - environment and possible change of mat. Put the mat by the back door practice a couple of times there, then put them out for a wee in the garden and when you let them back in give them the command to wipe as they approach the doorway/mat – if they get it straight away have a massive party! Tons of praise and rewards. If they do not, don't worry too much – it's now different to the dog and not normally part of that routine. Practice again without letting them into the garden for a couple of times and try again the next time you let them out for a wee. Once you have this consistently (success coming in from the garden around 5 times consecutively) then you can look at getting a better quality mat if you like and remember to practice this step again with the new mat.

Well done!!!

You can also use this kind of training (minus the twist/twirl) to help keep dogs nails short with a sheet of sandpaper – particularly useful for dogs who dislike their nails being cut or their paws being held.

An alternative to a door mat would be to do this with a towel too.

Be useful! Fetch carry and find!

Pick up and carry items - easiest with Retrievers, Labs, Spaniels, Gundogs.

Teaching your dog how to fetch will make both of your lives easier! Not just fetching balls but other items too, your shoes, something you have dropped, eventually this can turn into finding your glove or keys that you have lost on a walk.

First, we have to teach the dog how to hold/carry items before we assign a task while they are holding an item.

Pick an item that your dog will naturally hold in its mouth that isn't food or a chew. Their favourite toy or maybe a sock!

One of mine barely holds anything in his mouth but will always be happy to carry one of my socks around (he does not chew them or attempt to eat them. You know your dog best!) Ideally this should be something that your dog has picked up in its mouth before and not something that it is likely to run off with in expectation of you chasing it or try to eat it.

Give them the item, for ease while I take you through the steps, let's call it a ball (but you can replace with most things that are not going to be harmful to your dog).

*If you have a ball obsessed dog then this isn't the best item to use as your dog will be expecting a very different game and be too excited to train with a ball present at this stage.

Step 1 – sit on a chair with the ball/item in your hand, call your dog over and offer it to them. If they take it and hold it in their mouth, fuss them and physically praise them all over while talking to them and telling them how wonderful they are, good dog oh what a clever pooch etc. the whole time they are holding the item. If they drop it, immediately stop giving all affection and start again (picking up the toy and offering it to them again). DO NOT TOUCH THEIR HEAD or THE ITEM at any point while your dog holds it at this stage. After a few minutes you will find your dog will likely just drop the item naturally – this is fine.

Repeat 6 times with the dog holding the item for a minimum of 15 seconds each time.

*Troubleshooting: If your dog is avoiding you and your attention by moving away with the item – use a different item, this item is seen as too valuable by your dog and may be anticipating you chasing after them if you have before when they have stolen things. Do not restrain them while giving them attention for holding the item.

What we are teaching is the best place to be when they have something in their mouth is by you and that they have to be in your space bubble to get attention and praise.

Step 2 – repeat step 1 while introducing the word 'hold it' 'take it' or 'pick up' as you offer the item. You should see a pattern of when your dog will naturally drop the item by now so introduce a 'drop' or 'give' command as they are about to drop the item. *Please do not use 'leave' for this.

Repeat 6 times with both commands.

Step 3 – place the item on the floor between your feet, say 'hold it' or the command you have been using in step 2. Your dog should pick up the item and come into your space in anticipation of lots of fuss and attention as before – keep up this amount of physical and verbal praise as before. Be sure to use the drop command as you predict when they will naturally drop it. Repeat 6 times.

Take a break come back to this in another session.

Revisit step 3 and repeat 3 times.

Step 4 – place the item a foot or two away from you (within your reach while you are still sitting). Practice your dog taking a few small steps toward you with the item. * Do not throw the item – just place it on the floor. Repeat 3 times at the same distance before doubling the distance (you will need to get up out of your chair for this stage) and repeat a further 3 times. Remember to keep up the physical praise each time.

Step 5 – repeat step 4 increasing the distance again, when they return to you with the item, give physical praise but instead of asking them to drop the item after at least 15 seconds of attention then gently place your hand on the item (do not pull it or put pressure on the item) and give the command to give/drop. Your dog should release the item willingly into your hand. Give physical praise again for at least 15 seconds. Repeat 6 times.

Step 6 – you can start to throw the item a short distance while repeating step 5. Repeat 6 times. Take a break. Revisit step 5 (no throwing). Now practice steps 5 and 6 while you are standing up in front of the same chair.

Step 7 - practice again while standing in another room - repeat 6 times.

Step 8 - practice in the garden – repeat 6 times.

Take a break.

Step 9 - start to reduce your physical praise gradually while practicing around the house and garden, gradually increasing the distance.

Step 10 - practice on walks but only 3 times each walk – some dogs will start to get bored of doing this so stopping before they have chance to get it wrong or stop fetching the item is key. Over time, many walks and with practice you can increase this to 5 times and 8 times etc. The key is to remove the item/ball when they are still eager to do more.

You should increase the praise again when you start doing this on walks as they will need to be rewarded more around distractions such as interesting smells on walks. You can gradually decrease this again over time.

This is fairly hard for a lot of dogs if they are not bred to fetch and carry like Labradors and Spaniels are – though some Labs and Spaniels don't like to do this either so big pats on the back to you!

Massive well done!

Pick up anything – save your back! Or an excuse to be lazy

Now we have taught your dog how to fetch one item we start to introduce other items.

Step 1 - start by randomly dropping a different item at your feet when you are sat on the sofa or your comfy chair. Something like a reading glasses case or the remote control and ask your dog to 'pick it up' or 'hold it' if they do repeat step 2 from before! Loads of fuss and praise! And repeat 3 times. If they don't, don't worry! Simply hold the item in your hand and ask them to hold as in step 2 from before – repeat 3 times and then drop the item to the floor repeating 3 times before progressing to the next stage.

Step 2 - practice with 2 different items on the floor by your feet repeating a few times before placing these items further away and repeating again.

Step 3 - randomly throughout the day drop something and ask your dog to pick it up for you.

Lots of fuss and attention when they do! Once you have done this with success with 3 further items without issue you can progress to the next step.

*Note that things with metal on such as your keys etc. are harder for your dog to pick up as it's not very nice sensation against their teeth… you may need to work up to this! If you do want them to pick up your keys, then thing about putting a leather or plush toy key ring on them to help your dog.

Once you have trained this it's brilliant for if you have a bad back or knees as your dog can help save you some of the bending down.

Teach them to search for it!

Think about things you are likely to want your dog to fetch or find for you.
Examples may be – your gloves, your keys, your slippers, your phone, your wallet etc.

Step 1 - start to label items or give them a name, practice with one item dropping to the floor and in place of saying pick it up or hold etc. say the name of the item and practice as before, lots of praise. Repeat 3 times before changing to a different item and repeating this step again.

*you may need to say 'glove' then 'hold' a few times if your dog is struggling, after a few repetitions you can start to just say the name of the item and not bother with the command to pick it up as they start to get it.

Step 2 - have both the items at your feet – for example, glove and wallet and ask for wallet. If your dog gets the right one – have a party with them! Repeat the same for 3 times before asking for the other.

* If your dog gets it wrong don't worry, revisit the previous step a few times before presenting them with both items and trying again.

Step 3 - build on the previous steps with 3 different and labelled items, ensuring your dog is getting the right thing each time.

Step 4 - place the 3 items further away from you and practice asking for each item randomly, sometime asking for the same thing twice in a row.

Take a break and come back to it next time.

Practice step 4 again.

Step 5 - choose one item of the 3 you have labelled and hide it somewhere in the house, don't make it too hard. This will be easier if you have already been working on the find it exercise from the previous chapter. Place the item somewhere semi visible while your dog it out of the room, let them in the room and say 'find wallet' or whatever the item is. Initially you may need to almost show them where the item is and then move backwards a few steps, so they pick up the item and follow you to bring you the item. Lots of physical and verbal praise as before. Repeat this 3 times before practicing with each of the other 2 items individually as you have with the first item.

Step 6 - hide all 3 items in the same room and practice find it as before asking for each items individually repeat this 3 times.

Step 7 - hide the items as before in the room that you normally relax in, the lounge for example – while your dog is out of the room. Let your dog into the room and sit in your favourite spot before asking your dog to find wallet, then find gloves etc. This means you will not be guiding them, and they are going to fetch them to you. Repeat 3 times with each item.

Take a break.

Revisit step 7 just once with each item before continuing.

Step 8 - hide items in another room and send your dog to find the items while you are sitting in your comfy seat. If your dog struggles as they may only be looking the same room initially you may need to go with them to help show them where the item is. Repeat with more than one item with success out of the room 3 times.

You are now at the stage where you can ask your dog to go and get things! They can be useful! Massive congratulations!

Want to take it a step further?

Here is a bonus step!

Step 9 - take it on the road! When you are out with your dog on a walk, your dog off lead and ahead or not looking at you, randomly drop one of these items without them seeing. Walk on a few steps (keeping a mental note of there the item is) before calling them back to you. When they return reward them, then say 'find glove' motion with your arm behind you. You may need to go with them to help them understand that this game also applies while on walks – when they pick up the item lots of praise and rewards! Repeat randomly and building up the distance between you and the item each time. You can then, over time make it harder again by making the hiding places harder… in bushes and not in immediate sight etc.

This is great fun for your dog and also very helpful for when you have actually accidentally dropped something on a walk! I used to lose my van keys regularly on walks and I taught Merlin to do exactly this to save me hours trudging around muddy fields retracing my steps.

19 HACKS & ENRICHMENT

The time saving backpack walk

Only 15 minutes for when you are really pushed for time!

Beneficial to all dogs, particularly dog who may be a little nervous or who don't like other dogs.

Also great for young puppies who can't go out for a long walk due to soft and growing bones and joint.

What you will need

- 15 minutes
- A small space (no larger than the size of a tennis court) ideally a grassy area as you will need to sit down at times, but a quiet carpark would do the same job
- A place where your dog or puppy feels confident and secure (quiet without other dogs, people or distractions such as too much wildlife/bird/rabbits etc.)
- A long line
- Treats and treat bag around your waist
- Two Tupperware style containers – one with a novel/new type of food and the other with a novel/new scent such as

catnip or gun oil, lavender oil or clove oil – anything really that your dog won't be used to. Just a drop on a hanky or piece of cloth
- A chew
- A random object
- A backpack to put it all in!
- Oh, and not forgetting your dog.

Harness on dogs' body at all times that a longline is attached so they aren't jolting their neck if they go to the end of the longline.

Rules for you
- Only whisper, no shouting or loud voice the whole time you are on the walk
- Phone away and in the bag on silent
- Calm and slow mind set

Step 1 - ruck sack on your back, long line attached to harness on your dog (you are holding the end) and treat bag attached to your pocket or waist. Enter the chosen space and allow your dog to sniff, toilet etc. for a few minutes. If your dog goes to the end of the longline just slow to a stop make a noise (quietly) to encourage your dog to check back to look at you, when they do, calmly and slowly throw a treat in the opposite direction but nearby to you (this is most likely to be just behind you as the dog will be in front of you).

Step 2 - practice – 'Triangle Recalls' dog nearby, drop a treat at your feet and jog or run backwards away from the dog to encourage them to follow once they have had the treat (always within the length of the longline), whisper a call to them if necessary. When they reach you, drop another treat at your feet and repeat in the triangular shape. Repeat a few times.

Step 3 - now sit down, take a breather. This step is done slowly and calmly. Remove your bag from your back and deliberately open it (with a bit of thespian flair if you can). Pretend there is the most exciting thing in the world in the bag 'oh wow' 'oh my god, amazing!' 'I can't believe it' etc. while your dog doesn't understand what you are saying they do understand your tone and can read your emotions

– go for an Oscar with it if you can!

Take out the tub with the scent. Hold it gently as if you are holding a one week old puppy, precious and fragile. Give it lots of attention, for if the dog wasn't interested before he will be now. Slowly open the tub by a crack, allow the dog a sniff, maybe sniff it yourself – still treating it like it's precious and fragile. Close the tub slowly and carefully place it back in the bag slowly and purposefully – don't rush any of this, the better of an actor you can be the more the dog will be interested.

Step 4 - now in the same way take out the random object (this could be a length of plastic pipe, it could be a watch – ANYTHING) treating it like it's made of gold and diamonds, precious and fragile just like you did with the scent, now let the dog sniff, lick it or hold it. Return it to the back purposefully and slowly as before.

Step 5 - now again in the same manner slowly take out the tub with the food in. Open it slowly and allow your dog to sniff it. You sniff it too – make an mmm sound. Feed it in little bits, maybe share it depending what it is. Return the tub to your bag leaving a little left in the tub – again slowly and like it's made of thin glass.

Step 6 - now comes the chew – in the same manner as before removing it from the bag and offer it to your dog. Remember chewing is calming and your dog should lay down to chew it by you. Sit close and stroke him slowly while he chews but only if he is relaxed with you doing this. If he isn't just be close by and breath deep and calm – maybe sigh and yawn a few times to help your dog understand this is a calm and relaxing time together. If your dog is ok with being stroked while chewing, do not touch his head or the chew, try to stick to their back, and back end with your slow and gentle strokes.

Step 7 - place the bag back on your back and slowly wander back from your walk using the same route you came.

Remember this is about being calm and connected – not rushed or frustrated. Merely being in the moment and enjoying quality time with your dog.

Additional hacks while on your normal walks

Swimming

Swimming for dogs is great exercise, using every muscle in their bodies, just like with us!

Just 10 minutes of swimming can ensure your dog is just as tired as they would be on an hours walk! If your dog loves swimming, then if you can take them more often.

Be careful of blue green algae in summer which can be a killer!

Also be careful of not making your dog into a swimming monster who goes to find water without you. Ensure you put just as much thought into training them not to go into water when you are near it often, as much thought into encouraging them to go in! Distract them around water on some walks but playing with them or using find it on walks when around water and when you decide they are allowed to swim ensure it's only after a release command such as ok or go swim etc.

Swimming can be great to help arthritic joints – being mindful the water isn't too cold in winter, or your dog is left cold and wet for hours after.

Swimming is also a great way to exercise your dog on the hotter days in summer where longer walks, pavement walks and open spaces with no shade provide high risk of overheating and heat stroke to your dog.

Change it up

Find a new walk or go a different way around where you normally walk – what is it they say? A change it as good as a rest' Well with dogs a change is as good as a workout. A change in terrain, environment, sniffs and smells will also tire your dog out more in the same space of time. This is just one of the many reasons we vary where we take the hounds on our Hikes -variety is the spice of life!

Throw a treat for recall

With your dog nearby, off lead and on a walk call your dog back to you and when they turn to face you throw a treat behind you, let the dog chase and get it and each time your dog looks up to you again throw a treat in the opposite direction. Do this a few times before letting them go and sniff and run again.

This will increase your dog interest in you and encourage them to check back and look at you often.

Dog Parkour / Urban Agility

Get them to climb on things on walks – teach paws up/on, to jump on things and stay, to crawl under things to go around things.

Teach them to go around trees, to climb and sit on tree stumps. Ask for sit, down and stand while they are there then let them go and sniff or run again.

Mentally stimulating your dog at home (wear them out using their brain)

Training doesn't have to be tedious and time consuming – 3 minute training sessions are proven to be the most effective. Ideal for what the adverts are on, for when you're boiling the kettle or boiling an egg.

Raw carrots make excellent healthy, low calorie chews for your dog!

Primula Cheese should be your best friend! *Not the cheese and chive, or the cheese and chilli varieties.
Handy to take on walks in your pocket (let them lick a little direct from the tube as a reward for coming back, or walking nicely on lead), great for filling Kongs with, great as a distraction to towelling off, grooming or checking for that tiny thorn stuck in their pad.

Yanking back on your dog's lead is only making their pulling worse, just by stopping doing this and rewarding them for not pulling will make a world of difference (and save your poor arms).

The following habits with your dog are not helping!

- Saying walkies/getting your dog excited before going for a walk
- Pushing your dog down or shouting at them when they jump up
- Letting them play with lots of dogs on walks
- Leaving your dog's food bowl down with food in it all day
- Telling them off for destroying things in your absence when you return home
- Shouting at them for barking
- Letting strangers loom over them and stroke them on the top of the head
- Making a big fuss of them when you return home from work – particularly if you have a dog who isn't keen on being left alone
- Repeating commands over and over when your dog doesn't do it the first time 'sit sit sit SIT' etc.
- Practicing or training your dog to give a paw if they are a problem for jumping up in general

If you are doing any or all of the above, make a note of them, write them on a post it note and shove it on your fridge as a reminder to not do them. It's hard to break our own habits, so reminders are often needed.

Puzzle toys and chews are so valuable I can't actually put it into words! Not something I usually struggle with as I'm sure you know by now, I could type or talk for England when it comes to dogs!

Puzzle Toys

Kongs - I love these!

The invention of the Kong, the popular hollow dog toy which

has been on the market now for over 30 years, has been quite a blessing for dog owners, veterinarians and trainers world-wide. Its use is much more involved than simply being a toy a dog can play with for several minutes a day. Indeed, Kongs have been even recommended by veterinarians, trainers and dog behaviourists for behavioural problems, stemming from separation anxiety to hyperactivity. Kongs also offer great training opportunities, re-directing bad behaviours by offering a great alternative to problem behaviours such as chewing, jumping, and barking. There are many further productive ways of using Kongs. Dogs suffering from mild separation anxiety may be less likely to notice all the cues owners are about to leave if given a stuffed Kong right before leaving. Dogs in rescue or working dogs may feel more mentally stimulated and less bored if provided with a Kong each day. A stuffed Kong can be used as a great jackpot for rewarding those above average performances when training dogs. A stuffed Kong may bring relief and break the cycle in the initial stages of obsessive-compulsive behaviours. A dog recovering from surgery may be less likely to bother its sutures or itchy wound if provided with a Kong.

And these are just a few examples! Also, a dog in a class training situation that gets easily bored and distracted will benefit from having a Kong to work on.

Nature made dogs to hunt, forage, scavenge and work for their food—now we have made it easy for our dogs to find food; we deliver it free in a bowl! One reason dogs develop behaviour problems is sheer boredom, resulting from a lack of physical exercise, problem solving and outdoor exploration and investigation. To make your dog's life more enjoyable, you can give him fun "work" to do when he's home alone or when you can't play with him.

Food puzzle toys give dogs a chance to work for their food. These toys are sturdy containers usually made of hard rubber or plastic that can hold food or treats. They usually have holes on each end or on the sides. A dog must work to get food to come out by shaking, pawing, rolling, nibbling or licking a puzzle toy. The effort dogs make to get their food from these toys eases boredom, reduces destructive behaviour and lessens the anxiety they can feel when alone.

Start out easy - some dogs don't automatically know how to use food puzzle toys.

They need to learn how. When you introduce your dog to the Kong, you'll need to make it easy for him to empty it so he doesn't get discouraged and give up. Use small pieces of kibble or treats that will fall out of the Kong easily.

Make it harder - when your dog learns how to use the Kong and can empty it easily. You can make his job more difficult. He'll love the challenge!

- Use bigger pieces of food. Wedge chunks of fruits and veggies and larger biscuits inside the opening of the Kong.
- Put a few cubes of cheese inside the Kong. After stuffing it with the cheese and some of your dog's normal food, put the Kong in the microwave for just 5 to 8 seconds so that the cheese gets sticky and soft. (Be sure that the Kong is completely cool before you give it to your dog.)
- Stuff the Kong in layers; wedge something in the bottom end, then put a layer of peanut butter (only if sweetener and palm oil free), Kong paste, coconut butter, mashed banana or soft cheese. Next stuff individual small treats in and wedge some harder long chews in. Keep layering up to the top and then seal the top with mild cheese with something sticking out.
- You can give your whole dog's dinner in a Kong or Kong interactive toy.
- Hide your dog's Kongs around your home. Dogs love finding hidden food and unpacking stuffed food puzzle toys! Try putting your dog's breakfast in Kongs and hiding them right before you leave for work in the morning. Your dog will have a great time working for his meal while you're away. (A word of warning: Some dogs can make a bit of a mess while enjoying Kongs. If a Kong has soft or wet food inside it—or if your dog tends to drool a lot when chewing on things—you might want to give him

Kongs only when he's in his crate, outside or confined in a room with flooring that's easy to clean, like tile or vinyl. Or giving them frozen!)

- Make a Kongcicle! They're great for spring and summertime outdoor enjoyment. First, put a dab of dog safe peanut butter or soft spread at the bottom of the Kong to seal the small hole. Then turn the Kong upside down and place it in a cup. Stuff the Kong with kibble, canned food, cottage cheese, mashed potatoes, banana or anything else you like. Pour a little chicken broth or gravy into the Kong and freeze it overnight.

If you leave a stuffed frozen Kong with your dog as you leave, it can take up to a few hours for the dog to eat everything in the Kong. The jaw muscles will have been exercised, the licking of the Kong can calm the dog and the dog will become tired.

The list of what you can put in a Kong is limitless. Some ideas: cream cheese, leftover mashed potatoes, plain yogurt, ricotta cheese, cottage cheese, peanut butter (again without sweeteners or palm oil as these varieties can poison your dog), -- pretty much anything that's gooey. You don't have to stop there -- if you really want to keep your dog busy, toss in a few kibbles, treats, cubes of cheese or ham, chicken or liver and shake the Kong around so the cubes stick to the sides. Or, add some apple or banana pieces (no grapes or raisins -- these are toxic). I wedge tripe sticks or other long chews in so my dogs really have to work hard to get them out. You can put your dog's dinner in a Kong instead of his bowl.

Most pet shops sell Kongs and at first look they can appear to seem expensive.

However, they virtually last forever if you look after them (and not leave them in the garden for the fox to steal; I have lost a couple that way), so long term they are good value. Beware of buying cheap versions as they will be made of inferior rubber and your dog may be able to bite chunks out of it and could swallow bits with the food.

Kongs are dishwasher safe too, so you can safely put them in to clean. Take care to regularly check to see if there is any uneaten food inside your Kong that may have gone mouldy before re-filling it or it could make your dog ill.

Provide stuffed Kongs randomly so they won't always be associated with you leaving. If your dog is un-stuffing several Kongs per day, you should appropriately reduce the amount of bowl feeding.

Never leave your dog unattended with a Kong until you are sure that he uses it safely and appropriately.

Lickimats

As I have said before, licking is calming. You can get the normal range of lickimats in 3 different difficulties and they also do a deluxe range which has plastic backing for dogs who may decide it's easier to chew the silicon than to lick the contents. Soft cheese, peanut butter (no additives), natural yogurt and cheap sandwich paste are all great thing to use with these, you can also freeze them too to make them harder and ensure your dog takes longer to lick the contents clean.

The Snuffle Mat

I love this! And so, do my dogs, and my client's dogs. So simple yet so effective.

It may look like a very fluffy mat. And yes, it is but if we put small treats, tiny morsel of things they love into it, then the dogs get to 'snuffle' them out. It tires them out mentally. The thinking behind it is that is mimics them sniffing in grass, something that ALL dogs love to do!
If you feed your dog dry food you could hide their entire meal into a snuffle mat, really making them work for their supper!

If you don't feed your dog dry food, you could try some of the air or freeze-dried small treats in the mat; your dog's really will thank you for it.

This isn't something I would leave your dog unattended with as they may start to try and eat the mat out of frustration. So, this is a supervised activity only.

Nose down and hunting through the mat will help your dog focus and relax, the more they can use their nose the better – it makes for a very tired and content dog! This is a great thing to have for all ages of dogs, from puppy to old dogs, even when dogs age they still love to use their nose and it's often the last sense to deteriorate.

I often use snuffle mats to keep a dog focus downward when in a class environment or in a social setting such as a pub or café. Don't be afraid to take it on the road with you!

Once you are well practiced with the mat you can try scattering a few treats or their food over some grass in the garden or on walks. This is a particularly useful exercise for dogs who become excited or scared around other dogs or people. Allowing them to use their natural abilities to hunt and sniff helps to calm them when around distractions provided you are at the right distance away from the distraction. With enough practice you can start to work closer over time – though I cover this more in the next chapter.

Wobblers / treat balls

Toys that you can place treats in, and your dog has to push them around, so the treats fall out – these are great, time consuming for your dog, got keeping them occupied and making them tired.

Some can be loud as they bang against the kitchen cupboards etc. or if on hard floors so maybe only something for your dog to do when you are busy or not there, so you are not affected by the noise.
Do any of the following for 5 minutes, just 5 minutes each day. Or 3 minutes twice a day would be even better for just sparing that additional minute!

Quick easy games to play with your dog!

Find it

Hide treats around the house – perfect for rainy days or very hot days.

Shut your dog out of the room briefly and have some treats to hand; you can use either their normal kibble for this or some small dry treats, or a mixture of both.

Hide them at the base of your furniture, behind a houseplant, in a corner- all over!

Tip – try not to put treats on tables or on the kitchen side, we don't want to teach the dog to start looking for food in these places.

Let your dog into the room and say 'find it' you may need to guide them to the first few treats initially if you have never played this game. Once you have played this a few times your dog will start to get it, and know to look when you say, 'find it'.

You can also play this around the garden and use their daily food ration if they are on dry food.

If they are on raw food or wet food, roll the food into small bitesize balls and freeze, then play the game with the food frozen in the garden to minimise the mess and germs.

You can also play find it with your dog's favourite toy. Follow the directions above but hide the toy instead of treats. When your dog finds it, you can play a game of tug or fetch as a reward.

Hide and Seek

This game is similar to find it—but instead of teaching your dog to find toys and treats you'll train them to search for you. Like find it, hide and seek will exercise your dog's brain and give them an opportunity to use their amazing sense of smell. It can also help them come when called on walks and in from the garden.

Hunt for your supper!

Again, best played with dry food (or wet or raw food frozen into small balls). Measure out your dog's meal. Walk into the garden with your dog and their food. Hold your dog's collar with one hand and throw their entire meal over the garden. Release your dog and let them go and snuffle out their food with their nose from between the blades of grass. This will take a lot longer than eating from a bowl and will tire them mentally as they have to hunt for their meal.

You could add a little training to this by asking them to wait before being released (hold their collar until they relax and then release).

Strictly come doggy dancing!

Have a laugh; maybe shut the curtains so the neighbours aren't getting too much of a giggle.

Switch the music on and be silly and dance around the front room with your dog! Even if just for a song or two, your dog will always be ready to party with you. Mix it up; encourage them to follow you as you dance around back and forth side to side. Laugh and give them lots of physical praise.

Other enrichment activities

Cardboard boxes, ball pits etc.

Hiding chews, treats or stuffed Kong's in cardboard boxes for them to rip into and find. Or get small ball pit for your dog and hide these items in the pit between and under the balls for them to have fun with.

Egg box game

Take an empty egg box and some scrap paper and some treats.

Place treat on a piece of paper then scrunch up the paper into a ball with the treat inside it before playing it in the egg box, repeat until the egg box is full then give to your dog for them to play with and figure out how to get the treats. Great fun for them!

Muffin tray and tennis balls

Take a muffin baking tray and 6 or 8 tennis balls (equivalent to the amount of 'muffins' for the tray) and some treats. Place a treat in some of the muffin indents, then place the tennis balls in each one. Give to your dog to find the treats by removing each tennis ball.

Toilet roll tubes and a box

Take a small cardboard box and keep saving your toilet roll or kitchen roll tubes.

Insert the tubes upright into the box, enough to fill the base of the box, then place treats in some of the tubes.

You can make this harder by cutting up an old fleece jumper into strips.

Placing a treat on the strip then rolling the strip and placing the strip into a toilet roll tube in the box.

I'm sure you can be creative now I have given you a few examples. The fact is you don't need to spend a fortune to keep your dog busy and make them tired – you can just use things around the house!

Don't worry too much about your dog eating cardboard, while it's not something I encourage – it usually just comes out of the other end. The worst bit about using cardboard for these enrichments is the clearing up all the little bits of it around the area your dog has been doing these activities after.

How to create a place for your dog to dig

Dogs dig for many reasons. Boredom, to bury their prized possessions, to find a cool spot to lay in, and sometimes to escape. Often, this problem can be solved by creating a place that you can allow your dog to use for his digging activities. This solution is often less expensive and more practical than building a dog run.

Things you'll need:

- Child's sandbox or wading pool
- Clean playground sand
- Cover for sandbox
- Rubber dog toys
- Hard dog cookies
- Clicker and treats (optional)

1. Set up a children's sandbox for your dog. You may want to make one out of a plastic wading pool, but a plastic sandbox designed for the purpose is best. Fill the sandbox with playground sand which can be purchased at most home improvement stores and large toy store chains. Clean-up is easier if the sandbox can be placed on a concrete surface.
2. Bury dog treasures in the sandbox for your dog to find. Delicious chewies such as bully sticks, hard dog cookies, and rubber squeaky toys are all things that will make your dog prefer to dig in his new digging spot. This will make the flower bed somewhat less desirable.
3. After you have buried the treasures, place a hard dog cookie/treat/bone partially exposed on top of the sand box. Bring your dog over to the sand box and show him the cookie. Praise him for his interest. Or if you are clicker

training, reward all attention to the sand box with clicks and treats.

4. If your dog seems hesitant or confused, you may unbury a toy and squeak it to get him interested and then place it under the sand at a shallow depth to make it easy to get to.

5. At the end of the day, sweep up the sand that has been thrown out of the box and dump it back in. You may also wish to cover the sandbox to protect it from moisture and keep it free from cat droppings. (Though most dogs would welcome this addition to the treasures, we humans think it's really disgusting.)

6. Make the undesirable digging areas less appealing to your dog by spraying a dog repellent spray on them. You may also use bricks in the holes and/or cover them with wire mesh.

20 COMMON PROBLEMS

How to prevent and treat guarding

Does your dog growl at you when you approach his food bowl? Is your puppy possessive about toys and chews? Does he snap at you when you even step near him when he's got a bone? Does your dog bare his teeth when you approach the couch? If not, you're lucky! Read through this information and start working with your puppy or dog now, to keep him in the blissful state of loving your approach to his food bowl or other prized possessions. If you are seeing aggression, definitely read on to find ways to help your dog. The technical term for this behaviour is Resource Guarding, and it's an absolutely normal dog behaviour. However, it's not something we humans appreciate. Fortunately, resource guarding is also a behaviour that we can change.

A dog is an animal – no matter how we view him. Simply because a dog lives in our home and because we view him as part of our family makes most owners think we should be able to take a bone or any other item from our dog at will. We become easily affronted if our dog decides to become possessively aggressive about his toys – even more so than if our kids become angry if we try to take their toys away! But when our dogs become aggressive about keeping hold of their bones or toys or bed, the first thing we must do is not to see the issue as one of our dog engaging in 'point scoring' with ulterior motives of longer term control of his human pack, but rather as one of safety for ourselves. If we become drawn into physical combat with our dogs over possessions, as we will see later, we are more likely to cause ourselves a great deal of problems with our dogs in our day-to-day lives together than we are to teach them not to guard their toys or bones. Dogs don't have to be bad about sharing bones, but they don't usually love it!

Dogs, being predators, come programmed to guard resources that are crucial to their survival as part of their behavioural inheritance from their ancestor, the wolf. Some of those resources may be in short supply at certain times of year or in certain environments and are therefore valuable. It is beneficial for wolves and dogs to have the propensity to look after their food and bits and pieces against other animals including, sometimes, members of your own group. For example, this is usually not true for grazing animals in terms of food – after all, what's the point of arousing yourself to look after your supply of grass when grass is everywhere?

It's a huge mistake to label a dog with a resource guarding problem as 'dominant'. This is largely because it is just too simplistic to think that everything a dog might do which his owners disapprove of is some kind of a bid for power, especially if it involves threat behaviour. This label can also encourage owners to look for opportunities to score points back on their dog when their time would be much better spent looking for opportunities to teach the dog not to guard his possessions and to reward him for doing other things.

Here are a few of the myths about resource guarding:

- Myth #1: Resource guarding is abnormal behaviour.

- Myth #2: Because resource guarding is driven largely by genetics, it can't be changed.

- Myth #3: Resource guarding can be cured by making a dog realise that resources are abundant.

- Myth #4: Resource guarding is a symptom of "dominance" or "pushiness."

216

- Myth #5: Resource guarding is the result of "spoiling" a dog.

So, if the answer is not to "dominate" your dog or shower it with freely available food, then what is it? Simple. Make your puppy or dog understand that the approach of a human to his food, toys, space, etc. is a GOOD THING. The process is called classical conditioning. Just as the clicker is associated with treats in your dog's mind, the approach of a human hand, face, or other body part to his food dish should mean better food is on its way.

The following process should be done with ALL dogs, for their entire lives

Definitely do it with young puppies. The only part that changes is how often you do these exercises, what sorts of things your dog has when you approach, and how close you can get to the dog before presenting it with the treat. Every capable member of the family should take part in these exercises, keeping safety firmly in mind.

Initiate the Say Please Protocol with your dog. There are two reasons to do this. One is to inform your dog that you and your family are the source of all good things, and only by being polite does your dog get them from you. The second reason is for all family members to practice training with your dog, so that he listens to everyone in the family. This may or may not help with resource guarding, but it's not a bad perk! If certain members of your family are being guarded against, (growled or lunged at), then those people are the ones who should be asking the dog to 'Say Please' more often.

Teach your dog the cue GIVE. Start with objects that he does not value as much and treats that are highly valued. Then gradually work your way up to objects that he cares very much about. Ask for him to give the object, then either wait for him to do so (if he knows the cue) or cause him to do so by presenting food near his mouth. Reward and praise him for dropping the object, then give it back to him as soon as he's done chewing. Practicing this cue, giving the resource back each time, helps the dog understand that giving away his resources to a human is a good thing, so there's no reason to guard them. Children should only work on this step under adult supervision. Start with the family member that the dog trusts most (growls at least).

Teach your dog the OFF cue. If he is guarding the furniture, teach him to jump off it on cue. Get him up on the couch by patting on it or luring him with a treat. Don't give the treat yet (we want to reward for 'off', not jumping on the couch). Then say 'off' and lure him back onto the floor. If you use a clicker, click as soon as he heads off the couch. Give him the treat. Don't start to teach off when your dog is all settled down on the couch. Work up to that level.

Condition your dog to expect good things when you approach him, especially, if he has some sort of highly prized resource, like a bone. As with 'give', start with something your dog does not guard. Walk over, present the treat while he's enjoying his low value toy or food, and leave. Do this with several low value toys throughout the day. Repeat this for several days until he begins to look up at you, with a 'Hey, she's here to give me a treat' expression on his face. With the low value objects, move up to touching the dog in some way, grabbing the object (often saying 'give' first), then popping a high value treat in his mouth and returning the object. Over a period of weeks or more, gradually move up to repeating the above with higher and higher value toys or food. With high value toys/food/bones, start by just walking by the puppy, out of the range that makes him growl, and dropping a treat. Move closer as the days go by, if the dog is ready; never progress faster than your dog is happily willing to go. If the dog is not relaxed and happy at any stage, you have moved too fast. Retreat to the previous level. Repeat this entire process with several high value objects. After that, progress to doing this process with more people around, more stress in the environment. Children should only work on the conditioning step under adult supervision.

Keep your dog from exhibiting resource guarding behaviour by not moving past his acceptance level. If he growls when you get within three feet of his toy, then don't make him growl — stay more than three feet away from his toy next time. Better yet, remove the toys that he guards from the living area, so that he can't accidentally be triggered. If your dog guards his dinner, make sure no one approaches or give him his dinner in a separate room, for now. If your puppy guards the couch, try to keep him off of it by not inviting him up and/or by making it uncomfortable to lay on (an upside-down carpet protector works well for that). Any approaches that you make to your dog at this time while he has a resource should be on purpose and accompanied by a treat. DO NOT punish him for growling by scruff shaking or any other show of violence. All you will be doing is proving to your dog that he was right — humans are crazy, and you've got to protect yourself from them!

Maintenance. After your dog or puppy is happily accepting any human approach to his food or toys (a state that humans call 'normal' and dogs call 'strange'), you are at the maintenance stage. Twice a week, at first, then once or twice per month, approach him while he's eating, pick up the bowl, and plop in a handful of treats before setting it back down. Do the same with toys or bones as well. Occasionally practice the 'give' cue, replacing the surrendered object with something else if you really must take it away. Finally, continue the Say Please Protocol for the rest of the dog's life, incorporating new tricks as your dog learns them.

Oh no, he's doing it again! If your dog ever starts up again with resource guarding, it's not because he is trying to take over the world. It's probably because you haven't kept up on his training and he has started to notice that it's not such a good thing to give up his resources, after all. Remind him that humans are the source of all good things by going through the above process again.

Help my puppy is eating stones in the garden!

This is an issue I'm seeing becoming more common in recent years. I think partly it's due to us having decorative gravel, slate and stones as landscape gardens are more commonplace. Puppies explore the world by putting things in their mouths, there will be occasion that this will be items in the garden and of course stones being one of them. As owners we tend to panic as it is serious if a dog is swallowing stones and results in expensive and stressful vet trips and often operations which can be traumatic for pup.

The problem is mainly because we panic and often rush toward the puppy to try and get them to spit the stone out, this may sound strange, but it is normally this that leads the puppy to think that the stones are valuable and with enough repetition they will swallow them to ensure they don't lose this valuable item.

Calling puppy to you, distracting them with something else or even just asking for a sit or another behaviour will soon encourage them to get bored with the stone and spit it out. Try not to panic or make a big thing of it if they start to pick up stones, call, distract and stay calm.

Refer to the leave it training advice page 152 to help with this too.

Growling

Dogs growl for a variety of reasons. Fear, insecurity, guarding behaviour, offensive aggression, and play can all elicit growls, although to an expert these growls are each unique in their tone and pitch. Outside of play, growling serves as a warning that all is not well in the dog's world. Something is off, and our dog is doing us the courtesy of sharing that information. When a dog growls, most people would immediately tell the dog off or even worse hit the dog or punish it. It's human nature to respond negatively to a dog's growl. Growling is an undesirable behaviour and can oftentimes be a precursor to a bite. However, it's important to suppress your urge to correct your dog for growling. Thank your dog for growling and remove or redirect him from the situation that's provoking the growl. It's better than the alternative. Remember, to a dog growling is a completely normal and natural behaviour. To your dog, it is a form of communication. It's just that in our world we don't think it's appropriate, but it is to your dog and they will try to communicate why they are growling to you in exactly the same way they would to another dog.

Here are four things you need to know about your dog's growl:

1. **Growling serves as a warning signal** - it tells you that your dog is unhappy or uncomfortable. Something is wrong. Think of it as an early warning system.

2. **Punishing a dog for growling takes away your early warning system** - dogs who are punished for growling sometimes learn not to growl. However, getting rid of the growl doesn't fix the underlying cause for growling, which leaves us with a dog who is just as upset as before, but now has no way to express that discomfort except for escalating his display. The growl may be gone, but now you've created a dog that will bite 'without warning.'

3. **All dogs warn** - if your dog doesn't warn before he bites, it's either because you're missing his precursor signals or because *he no longer feels safe displaying them.* Either way, the fault here lies at the other end of the lead. Dogs that go straight to biting without displaying lots and lots of precursors are much more difficult to treat. I would much rather work with a dog who stiffens up, displays whale eyes, hard-stares me, curls his lip, growls, freezes, and then (finally) bites, than a dog who goes straight from a freeze to a bite. It will be much easier to keep the situation safe with the first dog. The latter case is much riskier.

4. **If your dog growls, he believes he has a valid reason to do so** – this may be because he is insecure, fearful, in pain, or frightened. Find out what it is that is making your dog growl. Treating the underlying cause will make the symptom disappear far more effectively than suppressing it.

So, behaviourally healthy dogs take most of life in stride, and they deliver warnings when they're pushed. Those two facts together help explain why it's best to respond without confrontation to a dog's growl or snap. First, underlying almost all aggression is stress - whether that's a huge stressor in the moment or an accumulation of small stressors over an hour or a day. Bear in mind that this is stress from the dog's point of view, and that many dogs aren't in perfect behavioural health. No matter how much you enjoy the toddler next door, if your dog growls at her you can take it as a given that he finds something about her presence distressful.

If you punish your dog for growling or snapping, you've essentially punished him for warning you that he's close to the limit of what he can stand. Second, if you punish your dog for growling or snapping, you've essentially punished him for warning you that he's close to the limit of what he can stand. If your punishment is perfectly calibrated, he may never growl or snap again. Now that cute toddler can pet your dog on the head, and he'll hold still. But he's not feeling okay about it. What happens when the little kid, who doesn't know any better, pulls the dog's tail or sticks a finger in his ear or runs up to him when he's eating dinner? You, the child, and your dog may well get lucky and go the dog's whole life without finding out. But I'd rather not leave everybody's safety to luck.

Instead of punishing, back off and think! - An outright dog attack is an emergency, of course. You must do whatever it takes to protect yourself or others. But if your dog growls or snaps, or if you've caught one of those more subtle warning signs I mentioned earlier, your best bet is to back off. Exit the situation. Take a deep breath or 50, enough for you and your dog both to settle down. And then think. What, exactly, were the circumstances around the behaviour? And can you identify any new or old stressors in your dog's life? You and your dog need professional help, and the best thing you can do right now is to gather information.

Remember;

NEVER IGNORE A DOG'S WARNING GROWL!

Stopping jumping up

When a dog jumps up, even if you glare at him, yell at him and shove him away, you are giving him what he wants; **looking, talking and touching**. Jumping up works! Dogs repeat what works.

Why do they jump up?

To get attention; to get you to look, talk and touch him.

As a puppy, this was irresistible. You responded by bending over and cooing. Now he's a half grown (or fully) over-stimulated adolescent and it just isn't cute anymore. This is NOT his fault; he is doing what you and others have taught him to do.

If we are to teach your dog NOT to jump up, we must concentrate on what we want him to do INSTEAD and spend lots of time teaching him and practicing under varying levels of distraction.

Your dog must learn to sit for attention.

If you or your guests pet your dog whilst he is on his hind legs, the behaviour of jumping up is being rewarded. The first thing you have to do is train all humans who interact with your dog! Teach your dog to sit for petting and then don't allow anyone to pet your dog unless both front feet are on the floor. IF your dog knows what he is supposed to do, when he starts to jump up withdraw all attention, including eye contact. Now remind him to 'SIT' and praise warmly, bend down to his level to help him remain seated. Unless you have spent HOURS proofing this exercise and everyone, he meets is consistent, he doesn't really understand!

Remember; the command is 'OFF!' not 'DOWN!'

'OFF' means 'put your feet on the floor' or 'get off' or 'off the couch'.

'Down' means 'put your elbows and belly on the floor'.

When you arrive home and your dog goes ballistic, jumping all over you, withdraw all attention.

Fold your arms, look at the ceiling. Ignore the dog completely; pretend there is no dog, no looking talking or touching. Dogs can be very hard to ignore if necessary, stand facing a corner and do not come out until your dog is quiet and calm. If the frenzy begins again as you come out of the corner, go back. The dog will soon learn that to get you out of the corner is to stop jumping and barking.

If you reach to pet him and he jumps up – withhold petting until you get a sit. If he gets obnoxious go back to the corner or leave the room.

An alternative to this is to replace the corner with looking out of the window like it is the most interesting thing in the world etc.

Practice, Practice, Practice!

Just because your dog will sit for you doesn't mean he will for visitors.

Practice 'sit for petting' as a stay exercise, daily. Raise your excitement level gradually, imitating actions of people who greet your dog. Waving – patting – goofy voices – squatting or looming – raise the difficulty factor in tolerable increments and help your dog succeed. Next, practice with family and friends, at the door after ringing the doorbell, with adults and children of all ages until your dog is fool proof. You will have to train the humans who come to visit as well, as if one in ten visitors' rewards the behaviour of jumping up it will take a lot longer to train your dog not to jump.

Once the dog knows what he should do, you can help the overstimulated dog resist the urge to jump.

Stand on the lead – with the dog in a sit, put your foot on the lead... there should be enough slack that there is not tension when in a sit, but not enough to allow more than an inch or two of feet off the floor. Bend slightly at the waist and extend your hand to pet him. If he jumps up, he will be unable to complete the jump. Calmly tell the dog 'OFF' as the lead becomes tight and corrects him and then 'sit'. Praise warmly and reward for any attempt to contain himself.

Step away – to the side or backwards suddenly as he jumps so he misses you, verbal praise the instant his feet touch the floor, remind him what he should be doing (sit) then praise/reward.

Excessive barking

If you want to reduce your dog's barking, it's crucial to determine why he's barking. It will take some time to teach your dog to bark less. Unfortunately, it's just not realistic to expect a quick fix or to expect that your dog will stop barking altogether. (Would you expect a person to suddenly stop talking altogether?) Your goal should be to decrease, rather than eliminate, the amount of barking. Bear in mind that some dogs are more prone to barking than others. In addition, some breeds are known as 'barkers', and it can be harder to decrease barking in individuals of these breeds.

Let's look at some reasons for excessive barking:

Territorial barking - dogs can bark excessively in response to people, dogs or other animals within or approaching their territories. Your dog's territory includes the area surrounding his home and, eventually, anywhere he has explored or associates strongly with you; your car, the route you take during walks and other places where he spends a lot of time.

Alarm barking - if your dog barks at any and every noise and sight regardless of the context, he's probably alarm barking. Dogs engaged in alarm barking usually have stiffer body language than dogs barking to greet, and they often move or pounce forward an inch or two with each bark. Alarm barking is different than territorial barking in that a dog might alarm bark at sights or sounds in any location at all, not just when he's defending familiar areas, such as your house, garden or car.

Attention seeking barking - some dogs bark at people or other animals to gain attention or rewards, like food, toys or play.

Compulsive barking - some dogs bark excessively in a repetitive way, like a broken record. These dogs often move repetitively as well. For example, a dog who's compulsively barking might run back and forth along the fence in his yard or pace in his home.

Socially facilitated barking - some dogs bark excessively only when they hear other dogs barking. This kind of barking occurs in the social context of hearing other dogs, even at a distance-such as dogs in the neighbourhood.

Frustration induced barking - some dogs bark excessively only when they're placed in a frustrating situation, like when they can't access playmates or when they're confined or tied up so that their movement is restricted.

Other problems that can cause barking

Illness or injury - dogs sometimes bark in response to pain or a painful condition. Before attempting to resolve your dog's barking problem, please have your dog examined by a veterinarian to rule out medical causes.

Separation anxiety barking - excessive barking due to separation anxiety occurs only when a dog's caretaker is gone or when the dog is left alone. You'll usually see at least one other separation anxiety symptom as well, like pacing, destruction, elimination, depression or other signs of distress.

What to do about your dog's excessive barking

The first step toward reducing your dog's barking is to determine the type of bark your dog is expressing. The following questions can help you to accurately decide on which type of barking your dog is doing so that you can best address your dog's problem. Think about your answers to these questions as you read through the information below on the different types of barking and their treatments.

When and where does the barking occur?
Who or what is the target of the barking?
What things (objects, sounds, animals or people) trigger the barking?

Why is your dog barking?

If it's territorial barking or alarm barking

Territorial behavior is often motivated by both fear and anticipation of a perceived threat. Because defending territory is such a high priority to them, many dogs are highly motivated to bark when they detect the approach of unknown people or animals near familiar places, like their homes and gardens. This high level of motivation means that when barking territorially, your dog might ignore unpleasant or punishing responses from you, such as scolding or yelling. Even if the barking itself is suppressed by punishment, your dog's motivation to guard his territory will remain strong, and he might attempt to control his territory in another way, such as biting without warning.

Dogs engage in territorial barking to alert others to the presence of visitors or to scare off intruders or both. A dog might bark when he sees or hears people coming to the door, the postman delivering the mail and the maintenance person reading the gas meter. He might also react to the sights and sounds of people and dogs passing by your house or flat. Some dogs get especially riled up when they're in the car and see people or dogs pass by. You should be able to judge from your dog's body posture and behaviour whether he's barking to say 'Welcome, come on in!' or 'Hey, you'd better hit the road. You're not welcome at my place!' If you're dealing with a dog in the first category, follow the treatment outlined in this article for greeting barking (below). If you're dealing with a dog in the latter category who isn't friendly to people, you'll be more successful if you limit your dog's ability to see or hear passersby and teach him to associate the presence of strangers with good things, such as food and attention.

For treatment of territorial barking; your dog's motivation should be reduced as well as his opportunities to defend his territory. To manage your dog's behaviour, you'll need to block his ability to see people and animals. Removable plastic film or spray-based glass coatings can help to obscure your dog's view of areas that he observes and guards from within your house. Use secure, opaque fencing to surround outside areas your dog has access to.

Don't allow your dog to greet people at the front door, at your front gate or at your property boundary line. Instead, train him to go to an alternate location, like a crate or a mat or to his bed and remain quiet until he's invited to greet appropriately.

Alarm barking is very similar to territorial barking in that it's triggered by sights and sounds. However, dogs who alarm bark might do so in response to things that startle or upset them when they're *not* on familiar turf. For example, a dog who barks territorially in response to the sight of strangers approaching will usually only do so when in his own home, garden or car. By contrast, a dog who habitually alarm barks might vocalize when he sees or hears strangers approaching in other places, too. Although territorial barking and alarm barking are a little different, the recommendations below apply to both problems.

'Quiet' training - if your dog continues to alarm bark or bark territorially, despite your efforts to block his exposure to sights and sounds that might trigger his barking, try the following techniques: Teach your dog that when someone comes to the door or passes by your property, he's permitted to bark until you say 'Quiet'. Allow your dog to bark 3 or 4 times. Then say 'Quiet'. Avoid shouting. Just say the command clearly and calmly. Then go to your dog and call him away from the door or window. Then ask your dog to sit and give him a treat. If he stays beside you and remains quiet, continue to give him frequent treats for the next few minutes, until whatever triggered his barking is gone. If your dog resumes barking right away, repeat the sequence above. Do the same outside if he barks at passersby when he's in the garden.

If your dog barks at people or other dogs during walks, distract him ***before he gets the chance to bark*** with special treats, like chicken, cheese or hot dogs, *before* he begins to bark. (Soft, very tasty treats work best.) Show your dog the treats by holding them in front of his nose, and encourage him to nibble at them while he's walking past a person or dog that would normally cause him to bark. Some dogs do best if you ask them to sit as people or dogs pass. Other dogs prefer to keep moving. Make sure you praise and reward your dog with treats anytime he chooses not to bark.

If your dog most often barks territorially in your garden, keep him in the house during the day and supervise him when he's in the garden so that he can't just bark his head off when no one's around. If he's sometimes able to engage in excessive alarm barking (when you're not around, for example), that behaviour will get stronger and harder to reduce.

If your dog most often barks territorially in your car, teach him to ride in a crate while in the car. Riding in a crate will restrict your dog's view and reduce his motivation to bark. Cover the crate with a blanket so that he can't see out. Some dogs bark in the car because they cannot understand that the car is what is moving, not the world.

21 DOG SPORTS & ACTIVITIES

Most people buying their first dog will not have any vision or idea of competing with their dog. However, you may want to, so I have included a list of dog sports in the UK with a brief description of each. Dog sports are addictive and expensive, but very rewarding and a great way to bond with your dog. They are not for everyone and most sports are not in the public eye and you may not be aware of. Have a read through, one or two may appeal. Consider this with your choice of breed and your lifestyle.

I have competed in Breed showing, Rally and Obedience. I have done all of these primarily with my Dachshunds but have also done some with my Flat Coat Retriever in the past. I have attended many training days for many sports to dip my toe as it were to see if it were something I might like to pursue and or my dogs may like to - for if they do not enjoy it then there is no point! So, while I have a good idea on most sports, I have asked others to give input into this. They are credited at the end of each section or sport.

Massive thanks to all for your help on this!

Rally

A fairly new sport, the first KC rally competition was in April

2013 and I first competed later the same year with Moss.

My first judging appointment in Rally was the following year and I am now one of only a handful of KCAI Rally instructors for this fun and welcoming sport. My Dachs are the first of their breed to achieve the top level titles (Level 6).

A sport which welcomes all breeds and types and is suited well to all handlers, including the disabled. A Rally course consists of various signs on a course which handlers and dogs navigate together, each sign with an exercise to perform. The lower levels being as simple as sit and the highest levels being more complex tasks such as control from a distance and formal retrieve of the handler's item which is placed on the floor by a scribe while the dog is not looking before the handler or owner sends them to retrieve said item.

The importance in Rally is put on loose lead walking and the connection between dog and handler. Progression through the levels is not through winning but from achieving 'qualifying scores'. What I personally like about this sport is that you are only competing against yourself, always trying to better your last score.

Level 1 is the entry level and achievable to most dog owners who are just starting out and have attended normal training classes with their dog. Rally is as much a challenge for the owner as the dog and keeps you thinking and on your toes.

It was originally a mixture of competitive obedience and agility. Whilst there are a few jump exercises still included they are under strict control and with a singular jump unlike agility. Many handlers in Rally do progress onto competing in competitive obedience and also in working trials. The skills needed for Rally are very much transferrable to other sports. Many handlers from other sports also then enter Rally competitions when their dog has retired from other sports.

Breed Showing

There are two ways you can show your dog.

To participate in Open, Limited or Championship Kennel Club Shows, you need a Kennel Club Registered Pedigree dog. If you wish to show your dog, ensure you go to a breeder who also shows and is doing well with their own dogs in the show ring - this helps you know they are good examples of the breed. Secondly you will need to research a local 'Ring Craft' class which will teach you and your dog about how to stack (stand) correctly, how to encourage them to move nicely, and how to work together to show off the assets of your dog. Avoid classes that use shake cans or spray bottles as these are not positive ways to train your puppy.

Shows have to be entered in advance, sometimes closing eight weeks prior to the show. On the day you will have to wait for your breed or group class. If you win your class, you will be invited back to 'Best of Sex' which is where everyone who's won a class in your breed (and gender) are judged against each other to determine 'the best'.

Best Bitch and Best Dog then compete against each other to crown 'Best of Breed'.

Best of Breeds usually then compete against other Best of Breeds at the end of the day for Best in Show!

The second option to showing your dog is open to any type of dog, pedigree, KC registered, crossbreed or mutt, and that is Companion or 'fun' shows. Each type of show chooses their classes which can vary from 'Best Pastoral' to 'Best Sausage Catcher'! You can research these types of shows on your local dog groups on social media.

With thanks to Jeannie G
http://www.putyourpawsup.co.uk

Scent Work

Scent work is a very new canine sport brought over from America. Tailored for all breeds and ages of pet dogs and their owners, it imitates the types of tasks carried out by professional handlers and their dogs in finding bombs, drugs etc. The dogs are trained to recognise specific scents and to search and find them. It is particularly accessible for 'dogs who need space' as the dogs work individually in class and competition. It is a great way for dogs and handlers to bond as they work together. There are a number of organisations both national and more local which promote and organise the sport. Scentwork UK is one of the largest and most widely established. Go to their website to find out more and where the nearest trainer to you is located.

With thanks from Karen Kendal of RBC Petcare Banbury
https://scentworkuk.com/

Agility (the sport with the tunnel and jumps etc.)

A dog sport that involves 1 dog and 1 handler to negotiate a series of obstacles on a course set by a judge to test speed and agility. Training and competing requires the dog and handler to have trained a selection of verbal commands and physical directions. Dog Agility is a perfect way for both dog and handler to keep physically and mentally fit. It's a great way to meet new people and dogs with the same interests.

With thanks from Stuart Doughty
https://stuartdoughtyagility.webs.com/

Bikejor

Bikejor is the sport of cross-country biking with your dog attached to your bike; it can be much faster and more exhilarating than Canicross and is particularly suitable for dogs who really embrace running.

What do I need to start bikejoring?

Aside from the obvious (a mountain bike, safety equipment such as hat, glasses and gloves), you will need a comfortable fitting harness for your dog, an attachment for your bike and a long bungee lead to connect you both.

Dog harness - the dog harness will take the pressure of pulling away from your dog's throat, which is essential if your dog is going to be pulling in front of your bike.

Bike attachment - the attachment for the bike helps to prevent the line from dropping into the front wheel if your dog slows down or stops suddenly. It is not a fail-safe but will dramatically reduce the amount of tangles you have.

Bungee line - the bungee lead is the shock absorbing element of your equipment and protects both you and your dog from the force of your dog pulling suddenly. When bikejoring, the line length needs to be longer than with Canicross to help ensure your dog has enough space and is running clear of the front wheel.

A brief note on bikes

You can start Bikejoring with any bike but one which is substantial enough for cross country riding is best. A basic 'hardtail' mountain bike is a great starting point. Brakes need to be good and many Bikejorers prefer disc brakes as for safety reasons you will need to rely on them!

How do I start training for Bikejor?

The best way to start your training is by training voice commands on walks, decide early on what your left and right commands will be and try to get a good 'slow down' command from the outset. You can use your line or lead to guide your dog in the direction you want them to go and also physically slow them down when you use your 'steady' commands.

There are no hard and fast rules about what commands to use and people often use different ones, but traditional sled dog commands are based on:

Gee = Right turn

Haw = Left turn

Hike/Mush = Go forward (starts or encourages the dog to move)

On by = To pass another dog or team of dogs

Straight on = To stay straight on the trail if there are many options

Easy = Slow down

Whoa = Stop

Things you can do to encourage your dog to run out front:

Use a higher pitched voice to signal you would like them to up their energy and prepare them for activity. It might sound silly, but dogs do respond to pitch changes in voice and if you raise this your dog will learn this means fun!

Go out in a group with more experienced dogs. Dogs learn from each other and will often naturally compete with their peers.

Get someone to run or bike in front of you. Again, dogs naturally like to chase and by having someone in front of you, they may be more motivated to stay out front. You can even use a favourite toy to encourage your dog to fetch it.

However, try not to rely on this method and always encourage your dog to run independently because it is not always advisable to train your dog to chase! Use the method as a tool and work on building your dog's confidence.

You also need to check where you are allowed to train with a bike or scooter locally, as this can be more complex than Canicross.

We recommend taking out some kind of sports insurance to cover yourself, when training and racing.

Some Forestry Commission land requires you to have a permit to train and these permits generally require £5 million public liability insurance.

The thing to remember is keep it short (at first), fun and safe, when you get more confidence you can then work on getting faster and even enter some races!

Canicross

The sport of Canicross is rapidly growing in the UK as more people discover it and the benefits it can bring for both human and canine alike.

Canicross in its simplest form is running cross country (on trails and paths, rather than roads) with your dog and many people have been doing this with their dogs without even realising there is a name for it, or that it is a sport which has its own competitions.

Why Canicross?

I've divided this into the 3 sections.

Behaviour - many rescued and high energy dogs have benefitted from participating in outdoor pursuits with their owners such as running (Canicross) biking (Bikejor) and scootering in addition to the more established outdoor dog activities. The effect of activity is to allow your dog an outlet for energy which might otherwise be used for destructive and unwanted behaviours around the home and garden. Canicross is a great way to exercise a dog who can't otherwise be let off lead due to (among other things) a high hunting instinct, which is why you will see many different breeds participating from terriers to malamutes.

Health - recent studies estimate that as many as one third of dogs nationwide are overweight and this figure is set to rise to over half of all dogs by 2022. Obesity is linked with diabetes, orthopaedic disease, heart disease, respiratory distress, high blood pressure, skin diseases and cancer (much the same as in people) so you might even be prolonging your own life as well as your dog's with consistent exercise!

Fun - taking part in dog sports usually means you and your dog get to socialise with likeminded people but even if it's just you and your dog, you will be strengthening your bond with your dog which is very rewarding and great fun too.

What do I need to Canicross?

The basic kit for Canicrossing properly is a comfortable, well-fitting harness for your dog, a bungee line to absorb the shock from any pull for both you and your dog and a waist belt so you are hands free when running. These 3 main elements form the basis for a pleasant experience when running with your dog. Without the harness you risk pulling on your dog's neck, without the bungee you can find yourself jerked after something interesting on your route and without the waist belt you may find your neck, shoulders and back ache from holding a lead.

What harness?

There is now a huge variety of choice for all sizes and shapes of dogs, with new products being brought out regularly. Which harness is best suited for your dog depends on a number of factors but K9 Trail Time offer a free consultation to help get you started in the right direction.

What line?

As long as there is bungee for shock absorption then most lines will be fine. Some are made from webbing and some from stronger polypro braid but which you choose is personal preference. The standard Canicross lines are approximately 2 metres when stretched but many people run with shorter or longer lines based on their own requirements. Some races have rules on line length, so do ask if you're thinking of competing in Canicross.

What waist belt?

The style of waist belt which you choose is down to what you would like from it and what you find most comfortable. The basic things you need to ask yourself are: Do I want something padded or lightweight? Do I want leg straps? Do I want pockets? Once you know the answer to these then it makes choosing a belt much easier. The purpose of the belt is for your comfort and to ensure Canicrossing with your dog does not damage your back, shoulders, neck or arms.

How do I get started?

The best way to get started is to find a group of people locally who are already Canicrossing, as there are many social groups' now encouraging new people to join them. A group will most likely have spare kit they could loan you to kit to try out and will be able to offer advice about training your dog with voice commands for directions etc.

Lastly, but most importantly, your dog needs to be fit and fully developed before you begin Canicrossing. Most races will not allow a dog under 1 year old to compete and it is recommended you start your dog off very gently at around the year old stage and not before. You also have to ensure you will be putting your dog's health first and to avoid any problems, stick to running in cool temperatures (never in the heat of the day in summer) and carrying water with you in case your dog needs it.

If you would like any more information on Canicross or equipment please do contact Emily at K9 Trail Time and she will be happy to help you. There is also a lot of information on her website www.k9trailtime.com

Canicross and Bikejor information are both provided by and with many thanks to Emily Thomas

Hoopers

Hoopers is a low impact, low cost, fun activity that any dog can try. The dogs will pass through a series of hoops, around or past barrels and through tunnels. The hoop and barrel size are standard across most countries, the tunnels used in European style hoopers are 80cm diameter and 100-300cm long, rather than agility tunnels that are 60cm diameter and 300-500cm long.

Classes are mainly split into the following categories', Hoopers which is purely hoops. Barrelers which is predominantly barrels, Tunnelers which is mainly tunnels and Mixed which is hoops, barrels and tunnels. There is no jumping involved in any of the categories, which is what adds to the appeal. Hoopers helps with the dog's proprioception. Builds teamwork and trust between dog handler, provides both mental and physical exercise and most importantly is fun for dogs and their handlers.

Hoopers is one of these most inclusive sports you can try with your dog. Hoopers can be tried by any age handler and dog team, you can handle from a distance or move more with your dog which ever style works for the team Hoopers is open to all. From Dachshunds to Danes any breed can try Hoopers. Younger dogs can start to build confidence and improve their listening skills; it's a great way to teach direction and to give your dog a job. Hoopers provides mental and physical stimulation so is also appealing to those with older dogs that may not be able to compete at other dog sports due to the intensity. Elements of Hoopers can be easily practiced at home or at the local park.

For more information on Hoopers please visit www.caninehoopersworld.com or visit the Facebook page @caninehoopersworld

With thanks from Carrie-Anne Selwyn

Dog Parkour

A great way to build a bond with your puppy and help them grow in confidence, while getting out and exploring the environment. Dog Parkour is a non-competitive sport where you and your dog work as a team for your dog to safely interact with obstacles you find on your everyday walk. Your puppy can step onto a kerb, balance along a low wall, duck under a tree branch - the possibilities are endless.

The IDPKA (International Dog Parkour Association) offer titles which guide your Parkour journey. You can work towards the initial, low impact 'Training Title' as soon as your puppy comes home and the foundation skills you learn will carry you through your dog's lifetime.

Contact details: dogparkour.org is the website of the founding organisation the International Dog Parkour Association

With thanks From Rachel Bradley

Obedience

You and your dog working together as one in a seamless partnership with exercises to show precision and accuracy.

It is the training that really gives you and your dog the fun and enjoyment of working together. It builds a close bond, great rapport, a high level of communication with each other and you learn a lot about your dog and yourself.

The competing gives you a goal or purpose to the training and it is just you and your dog doing your best in a supportive, inclusive and competitive sport.

Obreedience

Working with a team of like-minded people all with the same

passion for their breed to proudly show what that breed can achieve.

You are not alone, and team spirit is key. Training together and sharing knowledge to bring the best out of each individual dog and supporting each other. The dogs get to interact with the team, both human and canine, and importantly have fun and friendships are forged.

Competing gives you chance to proudly show what your breed can achieve as part of a team, you have support and camaraderie in a friendly sport.

Both sports above are with thanks from Jo Stanley - one of my lovely Dachtastic Obreedience team members

Flyball

In short, Flyball is a high speed relay race between two teams of dogs.

The name of the game is for each dog to pass the start line, run down a set of four jumps to the 'box', trigger the box to collect their ball and then run over the four jumps back to their handler while holding the ball over the start line. The next dog must not cross the start line until the other dog has reached the start line. This is called the 'cross over'. The winning team is the one whose four dogs complete their runs cleanly without errors in the fastest time.

In competition, each team will usually face four to six other teams in competition throughout a day that are of similar 'seed time'. A team's seed time is determined by their fastest time from previous shows or can be 'declared' but that's where it starts to get complicated.

The 'box' is very important. It holds the tennis balls. The most efficient way of triggering the box and collecting the ball is called a 'swimmers turn'. This is where the dog is able to rebound/jump onto the box using all four feet AND catch the ball. It is a very technical and elegant move.

A team is made up of four to six dogs, with only four required to run in each race, but can be swapped in and out between the six declared on the team sheet. The shortest dog of the four running is known as the 'height dog' as the jumps are set to that dog's level. A speedy height dog can be a team's most valuable asset!

In the UK, we have two main organisations that run flyball. The long established BFA, and the newer UKFL. Both have the same fundamental game but with slightly different rules making each organisation more unique, such as width of the jumps and how they determine the heights a dog will run.

If you wish to try flyball, it is highly advised you find an established and experienced team, as taught incorrectly, or too young, can have a negative impact on a dog's joints. Flyball is a very inclusive team sport but be prepared for the noise!

With thanks to Jeannie G

http://www.putyourpawsup.co.uk

Heelwork to Music

A fairly new sport which mixes elements of Obedience and Agility with your favourite music! Choose your track, no minimum length in time, but starters maximum music is just 2 minutes and 30 seconds, start playing the music over and over whilst training and put together a routine using your dog's favourite moves!

HTM is split into two divisions:

Heelwork to Music – where the dog does an Obedience style heelwork but can work on you left and right facing forwards or backwards and across your front and back in both directions! The music must be choreographed to show pauses, rhythm and different paces.

Freestyle – spins, weaves, jumps are the good base moves needed for freestyle. Match your dog's moves to the music and make your way around the ring having good fun! If you can keep your dog with you for at least 2 minutes, moving with your music and incorporating moves your dog loves to do, then you are well on your way to HTM success!

With thanks from Kath Harman for the information.

Man trailing

Trailing is really amazing; it is unbelievable how quickly all breeds pick this up. You start with short trails to find a person. The dog is offered the scent of the person to find. With that person visual, massive rewards from the found person. Moving on to longer trails person hidden.

It is great to watch your dogs do what comes naturally to them, using their noses. You are on the end of a long line with them on a harness; you fully have to trust your dog as you have no idea where the person is. You learn how to read your dog better. You will understand how they work, either ground or air scenting or both. Usually, they will use both methods. If you wish you can then move on to register as a handler with a dog that can help find missing people or dogs or just continue to work, your best friend doing what comes naturally to them.

With thanks from Sue Wood

Working Trials

A competitive sport based on the civilian equivalent of police dog work. They develop and test many canine skills - obedience and control, intelligence and independence, searching and tracking, agility and fitness. Trials are physically demanding for both dog and handler but are also great fun and extremely rewarding.

Working Trials tests are broken down into three main sections:

1. Nosework - comprises search and track exercises. The dog follows a track laid by a 'tracklayer' (who is a stranger to the dog) walking a set pattern designed by the judge and identical for each dog. The track is approximately half a mile long and laid on grassland, arable fields or heathland with each competitor working on similar terrain to others in the stake. As the dog follows the track it has to seek out and recover articles placed along the track by the tracklayer. The track is laid at different times, before the dog work begins, depending on the level of the competition. The other component of nosework is 'search' where the dog has to search for and retrieve articles placed in a marked area.

2. Agility - to test its agility, the dog must clear three obstacles - a three foot hurdle, a six foot high wooden scale and a nine foot long jump. Two attempts may be permitted for each obstacle.

3. Control - there are various exercises in this section which are detailed below:

Heelwork - the dog must walk with its shoulder reasonably close to the handler while the handler navigates their way around people and obstacles at different speeds.

Sendaway - involves sending the dog away across a minimum distance of 50 yards, the handler will then redirect the dog through a series of commands.

Retrieving a dumbbell - the dog must retrieve a dumbbell which has been thrown by the handler.

Down stay - the dog must stay in the down position while the handler is out of sight for a period of time.

Steadiness to gunshot - the dog is tested on its reactions to gunshot. The dog will be penalised if it shows any signs of fear or aggression.

Speak - the dog is ordered to 'speak' and cease 'speaking' on command by the handler with a minimum of commands and/or signals.

With thanks from the Kennel Club -
https://www.thekennelclub.org.uk/activities/working-trials/new-to-working-trials/

IPO/Schutzhund

IPO, formerly known as Schutzhund (literally translated as 'protection dog'), was originally developed as a breed suitability test for the German Shepherd dog. In the early days, German Shepherds were considered the ultimate working dog. While it eventually turned into a German dog sport, it has since evolved further into the largest protection sport competition in the world. Considered the triathlon for dogs, IPO is a three phase sport that tests a dog's temperament and physical soundness for work and breeding.

While initially only German Shepherd dogs were eligible, any breed can now compete in the sport. However, it's very rare to see a breed that has not been bred specifically for work to do well. Most commonly, you'll find German Shepherds, Belgian Malinois, Rottweilers, Dutch Shepherds and Dobermans competing successfully. These dogs have many generations of bloodlines created to maintain the temperament necessary for serious work. While IPO is a sport, the dogs it tests and promotes are used for police and military work. It is nearly impossible to find rescue dogs that can successfully compete and fight a perpetrator the way these dogs can.

The protection phase is the most iconic phase in IPO. It consists of the dog and handler team and a perpetrator called a helper. The helper wears a protective sleeve over his arm to keep him safe when the dog attacks. In IPO, dogs are specifically taught to attack the forearm of the helper. There are various exercises in the protection phase, such as a blind search for the helper and a full-field attack. Each exercise shows different aspects of the dog's mental stability and willingness to fight.

Protection is not the only phase in IPO. Equally important are the other two: tracking and obedience. Tracking is done with the dog following the scent of his handler or a stranger. The dog works at a 10 meter distance from the handler, and the handler must follow the dog as he guides him along the track. Depending on the level the team is competing in, the tracks are 100-600 paces and contain a number of articles the dog must locate. Articles are any piece of leather or other material that are hidden on the track. The dog must not only find them but indicate them to the handler by lying down. Tracking demonstrates the search and rescue capabilities of the dog, as well as his concentration and focus on daunting tasks for extended periods.

With thanks from

https://iheartdogs.com/dog-sports-101-iposchutzhund/

Disc Dog

Disc dog, which is also called Frisbee dog, is a type of dog sport which uses discs. Most of the disc dog competitions are distance catching and choreographed freestyle catching. A team of one dog and one person can compete in the 'toss and fetch' event. Points are awarded for certain distances.

Some of these competitions involve the dynamic freestyle event, which consists of choreographed techniques with music and with multiple discs on display. There are categories based on skills and experiences of the handler, but the long distance category is divided by gender. Some other popular events are toss and fetch, freestyle, and long distance. The toss and fetch is a mini-distance throw and catch event. The contestant can make as many throws within 60 seconds. The freestyle competition is a judged event, with routines lasting up to 1 minute and 30 seconds. The long distance event used to be just a half time show in the NFL.

With thanks from

https://www.topendsports.com/sport/list/disc-dog.htm

Pets as Therapy / PAT Dogs

This is not a sport, but it is an activity that you may want to do with your dog and it's a very worthwhile and rewarding way to volunteer with your dog.

Thousands of people of all ages benefit every week from the visits provided by our Volunteer PAT Teams, dogs (who have been assessed) and their owners who visit residential homes, hospitals, hospices, schools, day care centres and prisons. Volunteers with just a small amount of spare time each week work with their own pets, to bring joy, comfort and companionship to many individuals who appreciate being able to touch and stroke a friendly animal.

All breeds of dogs can become part of a PAT Team, they must have been with their owner for at least 6 months, be over 9 months of age and be able to pass the temperament assessment. Regular visits are generally appreciated, although our volunteers agree upon how much time they generously give directly with the establishment they visit. There is no minimum or maximum time commitment although our pets should not work for more than 2 hours at any one time and need regular breaks.

With thanks from

https://petsastherapy.org/what-we-do/

Working your gundog on a shoot and competitive field trials

On a typical shoot day there are three groups of people who all work together to ensure a successful day.

- The beaters job is to drive the birds towards the guns. They often have dogs to help them and most often these will be Spaniels (Springer or Cocker) although other breeds are often seen.
- The pickers up wait behind the gun line until shooting is finished then they send their dogs to find and retrieve shot birds. It is particularly important that any injured birds are

found quickly so they can be humanely dispatched. The pickers up use Retrievers (Labrador, Golden, Flatcoat) but again other breeds can be used on smaller shoots. Most pickers up work a team of two or more dogs to get the job done quickly and efficiently.

- The guns are there to shoot but often they will bring a dog with them. Known as a peg dog, this animal is expected to sit quietly while shooting is taking place then, when the drive is over, is released to find birds shot by its owner.

It is important that any dog taken into the shooting field is quiet, steady on and off lead and responsive to verbal and whistle commands. In other words, the dog must be trained to a high standard for the job it will be asked to do.

While shooting only takes place in the autumn and winter, training takes place all year round and in the summer months many people like to take part in Gundog working tests to assess how their training is going. The highest level of competition for Gundogs is a Field Trial, which takes place on a shoot using live game.

With thanks from Heather Harley

22 CONCLUSION

As a thank you gift I have lots of training videos and templates to help you and compliment what you have read, make sure you visit www.multidogmaven.co.uk/pupstarbonus to grab them if you haven't already.

Wow what a journey we have been on together! I hope you have found my guidance helpful and I have made your life together easier. If you wouldn't mind taking a minute to leave a review for it on amazon I would really appreciate it, that helps me to help more owners like you and helps to support my work for the future too.

It's not the end of the journey, especially for the larger breeds who take longer to mature than the smaller ones.

Training never stops, because learning never stops

Just because your PupStar is now 12 months does not mean you can sit back and just enjoy and never train them again. Remember they are still learning throughout their life! Whether you want them to or not.

They are still in the adolescent phase even past 12 months, it will get easier gradually now but don't just rest on your laurels.

Dogs are always learning, throughout their lives and often that can mean learning things we don't want them to do or finding ways around things to get what they want.

This is why my old lad Ziggy gets away with murder, he pushes little boundaries nowadays, and I let him because he's old and I'm soft on him. If I'm honest the little things he does don't really matter now because he is a good dog and doesn't cause an issue.

Always think about keeping the bank balance of positive experiences topped up. This will help with their acceptance of new or negative experiences and ensure they are resilient enough to bounce back and not become fearful.

Want to do it all over again?

Many owners often get tempted to go get another pup now, but my best advice is to enjoy what you have created together first and ideally you want 4 years age gap between each dog. It's so much harder with the next one, you may think it will be easier and you want a furry friend for your bestie to keep them company but believe me when I say it really isn't that simple! If you want to know more about the possible pitfalls and getting it right with your second, then take a look at my book 'Another pup?'.

Are you a breeder or know one?

I am always happy to help breeders and new puppy owners and ensure they start on the right path. I'm happy to offer stupid cheap breeder rates for copies of my books to send home as part of the puppy packs for litters going to new homes.

Drop me an email – sarah@houndhelpers.co.uk

Changes to come in 2021

As I mentioned at the beginning, at the time of writing I am going through the divorce process and making myself a new life with the dogs. This means I will shortly be using my maiden name of Roper, I will be updating the content and relaunching new editions of my book titles along with my name change, keep an eye out, I'll be known as Sarah Roper KCAI CD R QIDTI.

Future book subjects in the pipeline (keep an eye out for new releases).

Holidaying with your dog
Dog sport foundations
Preparing for loss
Lessons from a wizard/the goons guide to life
Fell from coast to coast
Loose lead walking
Reactive Rover

23 FURTHER READING & LINKS

Get your free gift – videos and diary templates to compliment this book here - www.multidogmaven.co.uk/pupstarbonus

You can find out about any new courses, books and talks by following me on the old book of face
https://www.facebook.com/SarahBartlettDogTrainer/

Another Pup? By the same author -
https://www.amazon.co.uk/dp/1720027161/ref=cm_sw_em_
r_mt_dp_U_fzWYDbRJ22MXD

Book one in this series - Puppy Prepared? The Roadmap to Getting Your Dream Dog
https://www.amazon.co.uk/dp/1707289778/ref=cm_sw_em_
r_mt_dp_0yvbGb29HBKXF

Raw feeding veterinary society for more advice and information on raw feeding –
https://rfvs.info/

Puppy Culture Exercise guidelines -
https://www.puppyculture.com/new-exercise-chart.html

Find a dog KC registered training club -
https://www.thekennelclub.org.uk/services/public/findaclub/

Dogs trust membership for public liability -
https://www.dogstrust.org.uk/get-involved/membership/

Guidelines for professional dog walkers -
https://www.dogstrust.org.uk/news-events/news/dog%20walking%20guide%20online.pdf

Find a dog sport -
https://www.thekennelclub.org.uk/activities/

WSAVA guidelines -
https://www.wsava.org/WSAVA/media/Documents/Guidelin
es/WSAVA-Vaccination-Guidelines-2015.pdf

VacciCheck (vet, in house, cost effective blood test for
immunity to three core diseases) -
http://www.vaccicheck.com/

Adverse reactions to vaccinations reporting -
https://www.vmd.defra.gov.uk/AdverseReactionReporting/Pr
oduct.aspx?SARType=Animal&AspxAutoDetectCookieSuppor
t=1
Worm testing - https://wormcount.com/

Dog food quality checker -
https://www.allaboutdogfood.co.uk/

Catherine O'Driscoll; What vets don't tell you about vaccines
book -
https://www.amazon.co.uk/dp/B00S8S7ZC2/ref=cm_sw_em
_r_mt_dp_U_SM-YDb81Y6FR6
.

INDEX

ABOUT THE AUTHOR

A qualified dog training instructor specialising in multi-dog households, reactive/barky dogs, and puppy training. A Kennel Club Accredited Instructor in companion dog training and KC Rally. QIDTI – qualified international dog training instructor. Sarah has been professionally training dogs for over ten years. Her company Hound Helpers Ltd was launched in 2007, which has helped thousands of dogs over that time.

She is based between Evesham and Pershore in Worcestershire but is proud of her Yorkshire roots. She enjoys spending her free time competing in KC Rally and Obreedience with her Dachshunds, doing various horse sports and activities including competitive carriage driving with her Fell Pony, Billy.

Sarah writes monthly articles for her local paper the Evesham Journal. She is also a monthly content contributor for the international magazine Edition Dog.

More book titles are always in the pipeline as she loves to help more people and dogs.

Keep up to date with what she's up to by searching @sarahbartlettdogtrainer on Facebook

She is often delivering workshops and talks around the UK too; you will find details of these on the Facebook page.

Author of -
Another Pup? The Comprehensive Guide to adding to or Becoming a Multidog Household
Puppy Prepared? The Roadmap to Getting Your Dream Dog
Joint contributor to the crate rest guide – Canine Brain Box

Printed in Great Britain
by Amazon